Sacred Space

Sacred Space
House of God, Gate of Heaven

Edited by
Philip North and
John North

continuum

Continuum
The Tower Building, 11 York Road, London SE1 7NX
80 Maiden Lane, Suite 704, New York NY 10038

www.continuumbooks.com

First published 2007
Reprinted 2007

British Library Cataloguing-in-Publication Data
A catalogue record for this book is available from the British Library.

ISBN: 0-8264-9477-3
ISBN: 978-0-8264-9477-1

Designed and typeset by Kenneth Burnley, Wirral, Cheshire
Printed and bound in Great Britain by MPG Books Ltd, Bodmin, Cornwall

Contents

Contributors

John North taught Ancient Greek and Roman History at University College London from 1963 until 2003. Having been Head of the Department of History for much of the 1990s, he is now Emeritus Professor of History. His research interests are in the history of the Roman Republic, in the pagan religion of Rome and in the religious history of the Roman Empire.

Philip North is currently the Priest Administrator of the Shrine of Our Lady of Walsingham; it was he who commissioned and organized the lecture series from which this book derives.

Jeremy Sheehy is an Anglican priest who serves as Rector of Swinton and Pendlebury in the Diocese of Manchester. Prior to that he was Principal of St Stephen's House, Oxford, and a member of the Faculty of Theology at Oxford University. He is a Guardian of the Shrine of Our Lady of Walsingham.

Michael Tavinor has spent much of his ministry as an Anglican priest working with church buildings of architectural and historical significance. He was Vicar of Tewkesbury and is now Dean of Hereford. An able musician, he has reflected widely on the theology of the built environment and is often in demand as a speaker on this subject.

Michelle Brown is Professor of Medieval Manuscript Studies at the Institute of English Studies in the University of London and a Visiting professor at the University of Leeds. Prior to that she was Curator of Illuminated Manuscripts at the British Library where she still works part-time. She has curated a number of major exhibitions and lectures widely on manuscript production and palaeography throughout the Middle Ages. A Lay Canon of St Paul's Cathedral, her publications include, *Painted Labyrinth: The World of the Lindisfarne Gospels* and *The World of the Luttrell Psalter*.

Timothy Radcliffe, a former Master of the Dominican Order and Prior Provincial of the English Province is a now a member of the community at Blackfriars in Oxford and a member of the Faculty of Theology. Fr Radcliffe is the author of many books of theology and spirituality, most recently, *What is the Point of Being a Christian?* He spends much time speaking at retreats and other gatherings.

Margaret Barker read theology at Cambridge and is the leading exponent of the approach to biblical studies known as Temple Theology. She is a Methodist Local Preacher and is part of the symposium on Religion, Science and the Environment convened by the Ecumenical Patriarch, Bartholomew I. She has developed Temple Theology as a basis for a Christian theology of the environment. Her books include *The Hidden Tradition of the Kingdom of God, An Extraordinary Gathering of Angels* and *Temple Theology*.

Eamon Duffy is Professor of the History of Christianity in the University of Cambridge. He is also Fellow and former President of Magdalene College. A Roman Catholic, Professor Duffy is an international authority on late medieval Christianity and the Reformation. As well as publishing works of history such as *Stripping the Altars: Traditional Religion in England 1400–1580, The Voices of Morebath* and *Marking the Hours: English People and their Prayers 1240–1570*, Professor Duffy is also a renowned theological writer and thinker.

Ann Morisy is a freelance speaker and writer who previously served as Director of the Church of England's Commission on Urban Faith and Life. Prior to that she was Community Ministry Adviser in the

Diocese of London. A renowned expert on the church's ministry in urban areas, her publications include *Beyond the Good Samaritan* and *Journeying Out*.

Sarah Boss is Lecturer in Christian Theology and Director of the Centre for Marian Studies at the University of Wales, Lampeter. A Roman Catholic, she is a leading expert in the field of Marian Studies and the author of *Empress and Handmaid: Nature and Gender in the Cult of the Virgin Mary*, and *Mary* (in the series New Century Theology), and editor of *Mary: A Complete Resource*. Dr Boss also enjoys making devotion to Mary accessible to the young and has published *Mary's Story*, with illustrations by Helen Cann.

List of Illustrations

Introduction

John North and Philip North

> All that a great cathedral can be, all the meanings it can express, all the tranquillising power it can breathe into the soul, all the richness of detail it can fuse into a large utterance of strength and beauty, the cathedral of Chartres gave us in that hour.
>
> Edith Wharton, from *Fighting France* (New York, 1915), p. 5, reflecting on a visit to Chartres, just before the declaration of war in 1914.

It may seem presumptuous to compare the small, 1930s brick-built church which lies at the heart of the Anglican Shrine of Our Lady of Walsingham to the colossal splendour of Chartres Cathedral. Architecturally and artistically they are poles apart. But the emotional and spiritual reaction of many who enter the Holy House in Walsingham does indeed compare to Edith Wharton's astonishment at beholding that great French church. How is this? How can so many people claim that a patch of ground and a small amount of enclosed space have the power to speak so directly and immediately to the soul?

The 75th anniversary of the restoration of the Holy House seemed a good opportunity to invite a group of people to tackle this complex and ethereal question. According to the Ballad published by Richard Pynson in the fifteenth century, pilgrimage to Walsingham dates back to the year 1061 when a widow named Richeldis of Faverche was taken three times in vision to Nazareth where Mary showed her the simple house which was the site of the Annunciation. Richeldis built a replica of that peasant dwelling in Norfolk at a site indicated to her by the springing up of a well, and by the late fifteenth century the

Holy House in Walsingham was the most important place of pilgrimage in England, attracting amongst its visitors every English monarch from Henry III to Henry VIII. Together with the Augustinian Priory that enclosed it, the Shrine was razed to the ground in 1538 and the carved image of Our Lady of Walsingham burned on a pyre in Chelsea. For many centuries the Pilgrimage was suppressed.

Then in the 1920s and 1930s, two Shrines were restored in Walsingham, one Anglican and one Roman Catholic. Central to this story of renewal was Fr Alfred Hope Patten who was appointed the Anglican Vicar of Walsingham in 1921, a man who committed much of his life to establishing the practice of pilgrimage as part of the devotional life of the Church of England. On 15 October 1931, the Image of Our Lady of Walsingham was translated to the rebuilt Holy House. Once again today, hundreds of thousands of pilgrims of all ages and backgrounds travel to that remote corner of Norfolk to pray in the House and to receive the waters of the well.

2006 was therefore a year of celebration for the Anglican Shrine; the marking of the 75th anniversary of that restoration presented an opportunity to explore the enduring power of Walsingham and the meaning of a holy place. During the course of the spring of that year a number of scholars, academics and practitioners were invited to tackle the theme of sacred space from the point of view of their own areas of expertise. The eight chapters printed in this volume were originally presented at four study days, each one held in a city or major conurbation, having some association with the Shrine. The first took place at Preston Minster in Lancashire, the second in a chapel converted into an Arts Centre in Cardiff, the third at Durham Cathedral and the fourth at the Royal Foundation of St Katherine in the East End of London.

All the contributors to this volume (except one of the authors of this introduction) are Christians, though they write from different Christian traditions and exploit very different rhetorical styles, ranging from strictly academic argument on historical issues to theological exposition, moral persuasion and even autobiography. They share a note of passionate concern with the issues raised in a discussion of sacred space. A central thread running through the book is the particular sacred space of the Shrine of the Virgin Mary at Walsingham, and the Holy House within it. Walsingham both asserts the importance of sacred space, because you have to be there to complete your pilgrimage, and simultaneously denies it, because when you arrive you enter the Holy House in Nazareth, not Norfolk; though, by another turn of the paradox, the Holy House does not pretend to be other than a replica. So the key themes of the book – pilgrimage, the expression of the feminine in religion, the relation between the particular and the universal, the incarnation and its consequences – all these themes intersect with the sacred space and with the ritual life of the shrine at Walsingham.

The idea that certain areas of space are sacred and, correspondingly, that other areas are worldly, is not of course a Christian invention but goes back as far into history and pre-history as we can reach by evidence or inference. Certainly, by the period in which Christianity was evolving, there was within the landscape inhabited by Greeks, Romans and their neighbours a network of sacred groves and springs, of temples and sacred enclosures, of wayside altars and shrines. The Romans in particular – that is the Romans of Rome, before they had incorporated the whole Mediterranean world – had elaborate distinctions between different degrees of sacredness and also elaborate rituals for the consecration of sacred land to the gods and for fixing the boundaries within which religious or political activity could take place – when consulting the gods, for instance, or making state decisions. The Romans also had a strong sense of the places made sacred by remembered divine action: the action would provide the material for a narrative or myth and a tradition of worship would be maintained at the scene.

On the other hand, pilgrimage was not a characteristic form of this pagan religious life: much religious activity was local to a particular city or area and, although there were internationally famous religious centres, there seems to be no question of any obligation on the individual citizen to visit them. There were famous oracle sites in Greece, Asia Minor and Italy to which you had to go to obtain the gods' advice; and there were deities, worshipped throughout the Mediterranean world, who had a special place of origin in one city, like Artemis of Ephesus, whose praises Paul's companions heard for so long according to Acts 19.34. Visitors to Artemis certainly went there to honour and worship her; they also went to spend their money, as the business fears of the Ephesian silversmiths in Acts 19.23–6 strongly imply. But pilgrimages in the later sense developed only in the Christianized Roman Empire of the fourth and later centuries AD.

If pagan dissemination provided one model of sacred space that early Christians would have lived with and known about, then the Jewish temple provided the precise opposite, with its aspiration to concentrate worship and holiness on the single site of the temple in Jerusalem, and the obligation on Jewish people to visit that single site on three occasions in the year. True, the destruction of the temple in 70 AD put an end to the actual worship, but not to the tradition of seeking a single holy place on which pilgrimage would focus. The temple in Jerusalem remained as an aspiration even though it had ceased to be a reality. Neither of these two models apparently appealed to those who guided the early development of Christianity.

It might seem tempting to say that the two models are simply expressions of the difference between monotheism and polytheism, concentration being characteristic of monotheism, dissemination of polytheism; but this would be to adopt a reductionist view of both religions. The Jewish God was famously not to be confined in a single place, but might express his power anywhere (see below, Barker, pp. 83–4). Meanwhile, Graeco-Roman deities certainly included some who belonged to a particular site, who acted and received worship only at that one site; but the major gods and goddesses had temples and altars all over Italy and, under different names, in the Greek world as well. Greeks and Romans accepted it as unproblematic that the same god or goddess could be at home in their city, given offerings of food and drink, paraded through the streets, taken to watch the games or dramatic performances, and yet simultaneously be at home in and active in innumerable other places. Their conception of deity, as in other religions, exceeded the boundaries of everyday common sense and accepted that divine powers could be both specific to one location and simultaneously ubiquitous.

The authors of several of the chapters in this volume are engaged with the fundamental problems raised by the idea of space being sacred: is there a specifically Christian conception of sacred space and, if so, what defines it? or is the whole idea of sacred space, as some have argued, alien to the true traditions of Christianity, appropriate only to the pagans and worshippers of nature? It can, of course, be argued that the universality of the single divine power implied by monotheism makes nonsense of the notion that any place is the site of a special divine activity. This negative view has been defended recently[1] and two of the contributors engage directly with the argument that notions of sacred space, and especially the journey to visit a sacred space, are incompatible with Christian theology. The counter-argument rests, as demonstrated by Sheehy in Chapter 1, on the theological significance of the incarnation, which, on his view, validates the particular as well as the universal. God participates in human nature and therefore the divine finds expression in the whole of creation, and consequently in particular parts of it. The Church has as its ideal to embrace the whole of human life, including its weaknesses, failures and sins.

Three contributions explore the idea of sacred space as it is experienced in different media. Thus Brown (Chapter 3) shows how the sacred is expressed in medieval manuscripts of the gospels, how the decoration provides gateways to prepare the reader for access to the holiest sections of the narrative. There is a clear analogy here with the preparation and revelation of physical sacred space in cathedrals and churches, where Tavinor (Chapter 2) discusses both the theory and the practical details of presentation, lighting and mode of approach to the sacred within the building. The third of this group is Radcliffe's (Chapter 4) treatment of the relationship between modern literature and the sacred, arguing that it provides a route for embracing the modern world in all its particularity, while still maintaining the universality of the Christian message.

---

1 This point of view is not directly represented in this volume, but see S. White 'The theology of sacred space' quoted below pp. 14–15, and for discussion of her views; but see also Radcliffe pp. 77–9 and Boss pp. 142–6.

There is similar parallelism between the two historical essays in this collection, by Barker and Duffy (Chapters 5 and 6). They deal with quite different peoples and periods: Barker with the Jews in the period of the first temple, before the reforms of King Josiah at the end of the seventh century BC, Duffy with the religion of medieval England before the Reformation. But the argument in both cases is that reforming enthusiasm led directly to separation from earlier traditions and to the loss of the feminine element in worship – the female counterpart of Yahweh in Judaism, devotion to the Virgin Mary in early modern England. Barker's argument is necessarily speculative to the extent that the female deity –'the Lady' – has to be reconstructed from scattered fragments of text and information that (so Barker argues) happened to escape the censorship of those who were able to impose their views on the composition of the Old Testament. Duffy can draw on far richer surviving sources, despite the success of the reformers in destroying the old tradition. Barker evokes a structural analogy between the house within a house at Walsingham and the Holy of Holies, as she reconstructs it, within the Temple in Jerusalem where 'the Lady', like the Virgin would have rested. These two papers, together with that of Boss (see pp. 145–6), raise the question of the connection, so widespread throughout Europe and Latin America and beyond, between pilgrimage and devotion to the Virgin Mary.

Much of this volume is therefore asserting or assuming that Christianity aspires to accept and absorb the world as it is, however sinful: but a rather different conception is implicit in the thoughts of Morisy (Chapter 7). She is more directly concerned than the other contributors with the practical problems of reaching the non-practising Christian, or non-Christian, inhabitants of today's cities. For her the urban world of the twenty-first century is full of godless distractions that divert people's energies away from realizing their own capacity for holiness. In her conception, the sacred spaces are the crucial way of establishing links for spiritually needy and deprived, even if outwardly prosperous, men and women. This is not to deny the implications of the incarnation, but it is to take a very different perspective on its interpretation. Morisy also shares with Boss the conviction that effort and suffering are inescapably linked to religious experience, though for Morisy suffering opens individuals up through their need for help, while for Boss it is the suffering of the pilgrim in seeking to reach the sacred place. Her theme is that of pilgrimage and its relation to devotion to the Virgin Mary. She strikingly describes her own pilgrimage from her upbringing as a Quaker, taught that everything shares equally in holiness, to her adoption of Catholicism, in the belief that sacred and mundane must first be recognized as separate before they can be brought together in a final unity. So she too finds the linkage between the universality of the divine and the specificity of space in the fact of the incarnation, and thus Mary is perceived as the link between the human and the divine, between the religious sphere and everyday life.

Like all good collections of essays, this one will raise far more questions than it can answer. Should the nexus of connections explored in these essays be seen as somehow inherent in Christianity as such, or only of a particular understanding of Christianity? Or are they no more than accidental conjunctions, brought about by historical contingencies? Are they shared with other religions, today and in the past? The next step in the exploration would be to compare the findings of these discussions with the ideas about sacred space of the other world religions and those of the pre-Christian world. There is also the question of the sacred in the secular: the 'hallowed ground' of Highbury Stadium; the wayside shrines created at the scene of a violent death; and that other famous House within a House, the *Big Brother* House on Channel 4, with its ritual of publicly expelling scapegoats. All these would provide themes for another route to assessing what is essentially 'Christian' about Christian sacred space and whether Christianity should or should not have a theology of sacred space. This book takes a first step on a difficult path.

Chapter 1

Sacred Space and the Incarnation

Jeremy Sheehy

It is often said that our society has lost its sense of place, of locality. In the past, it is said, we were a settled agrarian society where people rarely went far from their birthplace and often travelled little from their homes. But, some would say, the industrial revolution changed all that and started people moving, first of all from country to town, and then around the country, and finally around the world. In our age, mobility has again dramatically increased, it often seems. The report *Mission-Shaped Church*[1] points out how vastly more mobile people are today and notes how fragmented our society is. 'Most families, apart from the poorest, have access to a car, and are ready to use it. This means that people are able to work further from home, at the expense of having a longer commuter journey. It also means that at weekends people are able to do things at a distance from where they live'.[2]

We are, the report argues, a 'network society' and it comments 'in a network society the importance of place is secondary to the im-portance of "flows"'.[3] Yet this can easily be over-emphasized. A number of statisticians argue, I believe, that the relatively deprived are under- profiled in the government's Social Trends statistics (which are the figures drawn on by *Mission-Shaped Church*) and therefore those statistics may possibly overstress present mobility.

---

1   *Mission-Shaped Church* (London, 2004).
2   Ibid., p. 2.
3   Ibid. pp. 4–5.

And whether or not that is the case, the same Social Trends statistics also show that more than half of adults see their mother at least once a week (presumably this is only of those with a mother alive) and 61 per cent of grandparents see their grandchildren weekly. And even if people are much more mobile than ever before, that does not mean they necessarily welcome this mobility. Nor is it necessarily the case that mobility means that the sense of place is less important. It may be that increasing mobility has increased the importance of the sense of place, but people also feel an increasing need of it. We might also ask whether our social units are sufficiently homogeneous for us to speak in this country of 'a' society in the way the report *Mission-Shaped Church* does. I increasingly find I want to argue that within 'society' there are a number of different 'societies'. Some, especially the affluent in the South-east, may live in a fully-fledged 'network society'. Others seem not to do so. Place and locality are still impressively strong in their formation of people's sense of identity, I find.

I remember, when I was a parish priest in Leytonstone in East London, a couple came to talk about being married in church or about arranging for their banns to be called, and I asked the one who was not claiming the residential qualification: 'And you, do you come from round here yourself?' 'Oh no', said the young woman, 'I'm not local, I come from Canning Town'. Those for whom that is well-known territory will immediately get the point; others can either guess or refer to an *A to Z*. Canning Town is two or three miles nearer the river, the other side of West Ham, but only ten minutes by car and twenty on a bicycle. And many similar anecdotes could be told appropriate to different parts of our country.[4] People's strong sense of place and locality and the role played by that sense in forming their idea of 'who they are' surely help to explain why Lord Tebbitt's encouragement years ago to 'get on your bike' to those whose jobs had disappeared in their own communities caused such resentment and irritation, and also why it stuck so firmly in the mind. And in

---

4   Since writing these words, I have moved to a team ministry in the North-west and found, 30 years after the reforms of the 1970s, that the popular memory is clearly retained on the borders of Lancashire!

some ways our age has created new associations of place and locality, as witness the current fashion for shrines at the site of tragic deaths on our roads.

When I was far younger, reading for the first time some of the great works of literature and about some of the great events of history, I could not understand why banishment was thought to be such a dreadful sentence. Why was banishment often thought second only in its severity to capital punishment? Years in prison seemed to me much worse a prospect than having to live away from home. I was taking for granted the telephone and the postal service, even if email communication was not yet dreamed of; and I was yearning after the opportunity for travel. Kent's banishment in *King Lear*[5] and Boling-broke's 'bitter bread of banishment' in *Richard II*[6] failed to move me as they should have. Now, years later, I understand much more about the way in which banishment damaged the sense of identity of those who were banished. It is perhaps not too much to say that its severity lay in the fact that it took away part of their sense of identity, part of their sense of who they were, so that they lost something of their life. It was, indeed, a fraction of capital punishment.

Walsingham is a place of pilgrimage, and the whole idea of a place of pilgrimage depends on the acknowledgement of the importance of place and on a realization of the rightness of a sense of locality. We who value Walsingham are delighted that a Radio 4 poll has recently decided that it is the nation's favourite spiritual place. And at the centre of the pilgrimage there is a church, a place, and at the centre of that church is the Holy House, a place, an image of the sort of house in which the Holy Family might have lived at Nazareth. The image of Our Lady with the Christ Child sits in the house, but the Holy House was the central and original focus of the devotion and in one important sense the figure of 'Mary and her holy Son'[7] was secondary. It was the Holy House itself, the legend tells us, which Richeldis believed herself commanded to build and houses are

---

5   Act 1, Sc. i and ii.
6   Act 3, Sc. i.
7   From the Walsingham pilgrim hymn.

places, particular spaces, localities, particular 'spots'. Indeed, perhaps one definition of home might be 'the place where one feels most oneself'.

Many religions, of course, have had a long history of reverence for particular places, an acknowledgement of sacred space, and a consequent practice of pilgrimage. But when we think of 'sacred space' and 'sacred places', we must remember that there is a long history and heritage of Christian unease with the concept of the 'holy place', an unease dating back to the Hebrew scriptures, and which can be cited to fortify this unease for Christians in our own age. At the dedication of the temple, 1 Kings 8.27 tells us, Solomon acknowledged 'Heaven itself, the highest heaven, cannot contain you; how much less this house that I have built'. I do not think that we should ignore the seriousness of the criticism of our talk about 'sacred space' and 'sacred places' that springs from and takes strength from such sayings. How (it would be said) can one place be more holy, more sacred, than another? Is this not (some critics would argue) a sort of idolatry? Can one day be more holy than another? Can one place be more holy than everywhere else?

Our age tends, I think, to distrust particularity and to prize the general, the universal. There are, perhaps, a number of reasons why this should be the case, such as our understanding or misunderstanding of the concepts of democracy and equality, and an inability to see the role of the 'particular' as doing anything other than making inferior those found not 'particular'. This may be the case in our age, but, as many of us remember from studying the sixteenth century in history lessons and as every pilgrim to Walsingham must surely realize from the various ruins, there was also particular stress on criticism of the idea of the 'holy place' in the years of the Reformation upheavals. In part this was due to the undoubted superstition which the devotions at such places sometimes expressed and sometimes occasioned. But I do not think we should blind ourselves to the theological issues involved by convincing ourselves that a devotion to Our Lady of Walsingham or a pilgrimage to Glastonbury would have been found acceptable to the Reformers if they had been free from superstition. There is a theological discussion here that needs to be engaged in by those who would commend, to others still suspicious of it, a concept of 'spiritual place' or 'sacred space' and a consequent practice of pilgrimage. Not to engage in this discussion is to refuse to take the criticism seriously; it will serve only to increase the suspicion of those who make the criticism that such practices are not really authentically Christian after all. Bishop John Inge, in his book *A Christian Theology of Place*,[8] reminds us of the Reformation's separation of theology from the material and the particular. This separation, I think, grounds the criticism. He comments 'It became an axiom of Protestant theology that God's revelation in Christ broke down elective particularity, not only of race, but of place'.[9] As early as Gregory of Nyssa (331–95 AD), there were protests against pilgrimage. Of pilgrimage to Jerusalem, he writes: 'What advantage, moreover, is reaped by him who reaches those celebrated spots themselves? He cannot imagine that his Lord is living, in the body, there at the present-day, but has gone away from us (who are not there); or that the Holy Spirit is in abundance in Jerusalem but unable to travel as far as us.'[10]

Perhaps most of the early critics of pilgrimage are mainly complaining about abuse; but as well as protest, there is a theological discussion. Peter Walker, one of the biblical studies staff at Wycliffe Hall in Oxford, has written on Jerusalem and the Holy Land in the past few years in *Holy City, Holy Places*[11] (his D.Phil thesis) and in the more popular volume he edited, *Jerusalem Past and Present in the Purposes of God*.[12] Bishop John Inge suggests Walker is 'only prepared to ground holiness in people and . . . looking for support for this position from whomever he can find it . . . his is a common Protestant interpretation of the Christian tradition.'[13]

8   J. Inge, *A Christian Theology of Place* (London, 2003).
9   Ibid., p. 29.
10   Gregory of Nyssa, 'On Pilgrimages', in *Nicene and Post-Nicene Fathers of the Christian Church*, vol. 5 (2nd edn; Oxford, 1893), pp. 382–3.
11   P. Walker, *Holy City, Holy Places* (Oxford, 1990).
12   P. Walker, (ed.), *Jerusalem Past and Present in the Purposes of God* (Carlisle, 1992).
13   Inge, op.cit., p. 99.

Something of the same argument is found in Christopher Rowlands' essay 'Friends of Albion?'[14] He emphasizes how the death and resurrection of Jesus set Christians free from having 'holy places', just as the destruction of the temple in 70 AD did for the Pharisees and the rabbinic Judaism of which they had become the driving force.[15] Too often, I think, the commendation of concepts of 'spiritual place' or 'sacred space' and the consequent practice of pilgrimage has not seemed sufficiently theological to those who are suspicious of them, partly because of their Reformed tradition.[16] So we find the Reformed theologian, Joan Taylor, writing: 'The concept of the intrinsically holy place was basically pagan, and was not in essence a Christian idea . . . The idea of sanctified places, to which pilgrims might come to pray, cannot be found in Christian teaching prior to Constantine, and certainly not in any Jewish Christian "theology" that might be traced back to the very origins of the church. It would appear rather that the idea of the holy place is dangerously close to idolatry.'[17]

For such writers and in dialogue with them, it is not helpful to stress the ubiquity of the practice of pilgrimage in other religions or the natural sacramentality of the created world or the sociological reality of 'sacred space'. Indeed, because of the Reformed suspicion of 'religion' such considerations may simply increase the hostility, magnify the unease and supply new grounds for it. Consider, for instance, Karl Barth's comment that 'religion is the contradiction of revelation'.[18]

The liturgist Susan White, writing from a generally Barthian theological perspective, contributed to a series of lectures originally given at Durham University. Her essay in the published volume, entitled

---

14   C.C. Rowland 'Friends of Albion', in S. Platten and C. Lewis (eds), *Flagships of the Spirit: Cathedrals in Society* (London, 1998).

15   Ibid., p. 23.

16   It is worth noting here how strange it is that *The Pilgrim's Progress*, one of the most widely read books of Reformed Christian life, should use the idea of pilgrimage to a spiritual place.

17   J. Taylor, *Christians and the Holy Places* (Oxford, 1993), p. 341.

18   K. Barth, *Christian Dogmatics* 1, 2 (Edinburgh, 1956), pp. 303–3.

'The Theology of Sacred Space',[19] basically argues that the Christian theologian should not actually have a 'Theology of Sacred Space'. She writes about her unease that there has been so little consideration of the topic by systematic theologians. She comments that: 'The discussion of sacred space has by default passed to others than theologians . . . the work has been done by liturgists, . . . by people whose primary interest is the architectural history of church buildings, . . . by a few historians of religion.'[20] Evidently, she does not think much of this; she sums up:

> Generally the interpretation of sacred space they propose is taken over almost wholesale from studies of how sacred spaces function in tribal religions or eastern religions, sometimes (but not always) with Christian terms interpolated here and there . . . In general, there has been a lot of talk about ley-lines and mandalas, and poles of the universe and aboriginal dreaming-places and such. Some of this is intertwined with depth-psychology and semiotics, which no doubt is interesting to be sure, but it should not be mistaken for Christian theology. So the first problem is that up to now a Christian theology of sacred space has not been very theological; and the second problem is that the Christian theology of sacred space has not been very Christian.[21]

In response to this challenge and in search of a thoroughly theological and thoroughly Christian theology of sacred space, I would argue that the answer springs directly from the doctrine of the incarnation. Those who take the line adopted by the likes of Peter Walker, Joan Taylor and Susan White, may be doing so because they have not thoroughly unpacked the consequences of the doctrine of the incarnation. At the same time, recent attempts to commend the concepts of the 'spiritual place' and 'sacred space' do not, it seems to me, stress that doctrine's implications enough. *Flagships of the Spirit*

---

19   S.White, 'The Theology of Sacred Space', in A. Loades and D. Brown (eds), *The Sense of the Sacramental* (London, 1995), pp. 31–43.
20   Ibid., p. 36.
21   Ibid.

does not include a chapter on the significance of the incarnation, while John Inge's *A Christian Theology of Place* has, under the subheading 'The Incarnation', no more than a four-page section.[22]

At the heart of the Christian faith, there is the incarnation. God comes to us in our humanity. Jesus of Nazareth is the expression in visible, material, human terms of the character of God. God comes to us in the flesh, so that we can say that God is crucified and our human nature is risen and glorified. Now this stress on the incarnation has been a particular note of Anglican theology.[23] Dorothy L. Sayers, Anglican lay woman theologian as well as detective story writer and translator of Dante, insisted in all her writings about the Christian faith on the particularity of the doctrines on which it depends, on the particularity of the events on which it depends. In her notes to the Penguin Dante she comments: 'The Christian formula is not: "Humanity manifests certain adumbrations of the divine", but "*This* man was very God." On that pivot of singularity the whole Christian interpretation of phenomena uncompromisingly turns.'[24] And yet this particularity carries with it a universality. In Sayers' radio play, *The Man Born to be King*, Mary says: 'I, Mary, am the fact; God is the truth; but Jesus is fact and truth – he is reality. You cannot see the immortal truth till it is born in the flesh of the fact.'[25]

Thus the particular conveys the universal, and what is universal is rooted in what is particular. This appears to be a principle of God's working with us. It is expressed in the incarnation and, of course, it is a principle at work in the idea of a sacrament. It is because of this principle that at its best the Christian faith has been able to overcome the polarity between the material and the spiritual, the profane and the sacred, the natural and the supernatural. The visible and the invisible spheres of existence are not altogether separate, but are

---

22   Inge, op.cit., pp. 51–4.

23   A.M. Ramsey, *From Gore to Temple* (London, 1960), chapter 2.

24   D. L. Sayers in Dante, *The Divine Comedy*, vol. 2: *Purgatory*. (Harmondsworth, 1995), p. 39.

25   D. L. Sayers, *The Man Born to be King*, Act 11, Sc. 1. (London, 1943), p. 295. See also: *A Matter of Eternity: Selections from the Writings of Dorothy L. Sayers* R. K. Sprague (ed.) (London, 1973), p. 49.

related such that one is the effective sign of the other (in other words, they are related sacramentally). That is why Archbishop Temple referred to Christianity as by far the most materialistic of the great world religions.[26] The creation, the incarnation, the resurrection, the sacramental system of the Church, and the final glory of God's kingdom in the resurrection of the dead and the transfiguration of all: these things all express the same pattern in God's working with us. You may know H. R. Bramley's attempt to put this into verse in a Christmas hymn:

> The great God of heaven is come down to earth,
> His mother a virgin and sinless his birth;
> The Father eternal his Father alone;
> He sleeps in the manger, he reigns on the throne.[27]

In a later verse he pushes the paradoxes further:

> O wonder of wonders, which none can unfold;
> The Ancient of Days is an hour or two old;
> The maker of all things is made of the earth,
> Man is worshipped by angels, and God comes to birth.

I regret that the *New English Hymnal* compilers thought it best to leave out a verse which is not only a masterpiece of theological compression, but also reminds us that the shadow of the cross falls across the stable at Bethlehem:

> The Word in the bliss of the Godhead remains,
> Yet in flesh comes to suffer the keenest of pains;
> He is that he was and for ever shall be
> But becomes what he was not, for you and for me.[28]

---

26   See W. Temple, *Nature, Man, and God* (London, 1935), p. 478 – but the spoken remark was remembered by many.

27   H. R. Bramley, in *The New English Hymnal* (Norwich, 1986), no. 29, p. 40f.

28   *The English Hymnal* (Oxford and London, 1906), no. 29 p. 17.

Mark Frank, one of the Caroline divines, Master of Pembroke College in Cambridge and a man who seems to have been marked out by his contemporaries to be a distinguished bishop but for his early death at the age of 51, emphasized in his sermons the way in which the incarnation is the making visible of the invisible, the making particular of the eternal, and the making small of the uncontainable. In his Second Sermon for Christmas Day he has this to say: 'She the mother of the everlasting God; he God without a mother; God blessed for evermore. Great persons as ever met upon a day. Yet as great as the persons, and great as the day, the great lesson of them both is to be little, to think and make little of ourselves; seeing the infinite greatness in this day become so little, Eternity a child, the rays of glory wrapt in rags, Heaven crowded into the corner of a stable, and he that is everywhere want a room.'[29] I might also quote from Charles Williams, from both his fantasy novels and his theological apologetic, illustrating his concern for place, his high esteem of the material, his wish to affirm the affirmative way in the midst of so much praise for the *via negativa*, and the theological grounding of each of these in the doctrine and mystery of the incarnation.

Let me now try and relate this stress on the incarnation to the issue of 'sacred space' and the theological justification for the 'spiritual place' and for pilgrimage. If William Temple is right about the material and its high esteem in the Christian faith, the same must surely be true of place, for matter exists in space, and if God is expressed in materiality He is also expressed in place (with the same theological strengths and weaknesses). As Bishop John Inge says of Temple, 'There are far-reaching implications here not only for the *material*, but also for the *particular*'.[30] Now if this line of thinking is sound, those who say that Jesus generalizes the particularities of the Hebrew scriptures are mistaken: it is not that he generalizes them, but that the particularities remain and are given new meaning. The

---

29   Mark Frank, 'The Second Sermon on Christmas Day', in *LI Sermons preached by the Reverend Dr Mark Frank* (London, 1672), p. 53. Reprinted in the *Library of Anglo-Catholic Theology* (Oxford, 1849), Vol. 1, p. 77.
30   Inge, op. cit., p. 52.

particularities become sacramental. As T. F. Torrance writes in *Space, Time and Incarnation*:

> While the Incarnation does not mean that God is limited by space and time, it asserts the reality of space and time for God in the actuality of His relations with us, and at the same time binds us to space and time in all our relations with Him. We can no more contract out of space and time than we can contract out of the creature-Creator relationship and God 'can' no more contract out of space and time than He 'can' go back on the Incarnation of His Son or retreat from the love in which He made the world, with which He loves it, through which He redeems it, and by which He is pledged to uphold it.[31]

There is a parallel, I suggest, between the discussion of iconoclasm in the eighth and ninth centuries AD and the current discussions of sacred space. The iconoclastic controversies are, in a way, a consequence of Christology. How you thought about the icons was a consequence of how you thought about Christ. This is why some have argued (I think rightly) that the iconoclastic controversy was an instalment in the defence of the full human nature of Christ. Some said God could not be pictured. Others said that being 'picturable' was a consequence of the incarnation; if the incarnation meant taking on human nature, it followed that Jesus, if truly the Word incarnate, must be 'picturable'. Indeed, a refusal to picture Jesus Christ would look perilously like a denial of the full truth of the incarnation, an avoidance of the paradox of God among us, a watering-down of the full humanity of Christ. Christoph Schönborn[32] traces the conviction of those who defend the icons that people who reject them in principle also ultimately reject – if they understand the arguments – the mystery of the incarnation. The controversy was not about aesthetic ideals and about whether it was pleasant to have pictures in church, but about theological and in particular Christological

---

31   T. F. Torrance, *Space, Time and Incarnation* (London, New York, Toronto, 1969), p. 67.
32   C. Schönborn, *God's Human Face* (San Francisco, 1994).

fundamentals. In the same way, it seems to me that any understanding of the incarnation that takes its full truth seriously is going to
yield a theology of the 'spiritual place' and the 'sacred space', a theology which, to use the terms which Susan White used in the quotation
to which I referred earlier, but to reverse its meaning, is both thoroughly theological and very Christian. This is the understanding
for which the shrine at Walsingham stands, for Walsingham is pre-
eminently a shrine of the incarnation of the eternal son, and at
Walsingham we are reminded that God has dwelt among us, actually
lived in our midst, sharing our human nature – for here God has a
house and God has a mother.

Chapter 2

Sacred Space and the Built Environment

Michael Tavinor

Introduction

Which part of a medieval church speaks most powerfully of sacred space? Is it the altar? the font? the nave? the sanctuary? My vote goes to the screen – *de rigeur* in any medieval church, as defining and protecting sacred space and beckoning us onwards into space even more holy. In some Christian traditions, screens are still vital – the iconostasis of the Orthodox liturgy and the curtain of the Ethiopian rite. In the Anglican church of today, these markers of sacred space are, as often as not, a nuisance and irrelevance.

The metal Victorian screen in Hereford Cathedral, replacing an earlier stone screen, although not offering the clear division of Gloucester Cathedral or a York Minister, nevertheless did give some sense of division (Illustration 1). In response to changing liturgical styles, it was removed in 1967 and now, magnificently and expensively restored, it graces the gallery overlooking the entrance to the Victoria and Albert Museum in London. My question is this: is this screen, once an example *par excellence* of sacred space, still a symbol of that sacred space? Does its new position and its juxtaposition with a contemporary glass sculpture render it less powerful? Is it now just a wonderful example of Victorian metalwork and no more? Or does its new life ask us to re-think our concept of sacred space – in tradition and today? The first part of my essay looks at what made space sacred in the medieval period, perhaps the period of history which still most defines sacred space for us. I go on to look at ways in which

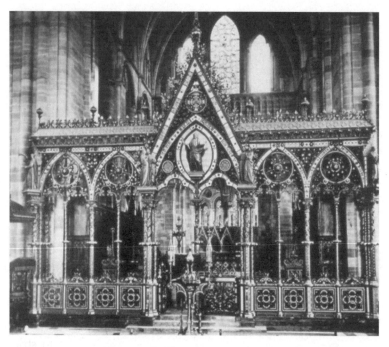

Illustration 1

The screen that used to stand in Hereford Cathedral. This Victorian version
made of metal, which itself replaced an earlier stone one, was removed in 1967
and now, magnificently and expensively restored, graces the gallery overlooking
the entrance to the Victoria and Albert Museum in London.

our traditional medieval concept of sacred space may need to be
modified in the world today.

Secondly, I look at the tension between sacred and secular in
sacred space. For me, this is nowhere better exemplified than in Hereford again – this time in All Saints church, just 200 yards from the
Cathedral. Standing in the church, facing east, we are on familiar
ground: altar, crucifix, medieval stalls. Facing west we are confronted
by Cafe@All Saints. About 3,000 people come through the church
doors each week, they say. What has the cafe done to sacred
space? Sacred space is often defined in terms of what secular space is
not. And so the second part of this chapter looks at these distinctions
between sacred and secular and how they have been interpreted in

church buildings over the centuries. First, then, the medieval period: what made space sacred in the medieval period and what lessons can be learned today?

Sacred Space and Geometry

The relationship between sacred space and geometry is vital in thinking about medieval sacred space. Today we tend to think of beauty as in the eye of the beholder. For Augustine of Hippo and those who followed him, beauty was rather more objective. Something could be beautiful if it exactly mirrored the geometric regularity of the divine order, and if it did, it had by definition to be beautiful. Chartres is the supreme example, where the builders embraced the sacredness of geometry and the aesthetic consequences of exposure to it. They believed that geometry was a means of linking human beings to God, that mathematics was a vehicle for revealing to humankind the innermost secrets of heaven. This could lead to disastrous consequences, of course. Because builders aspired to model their structures on divine order they assumed that, as long as they kept to strict geometric principles, their buildings would be structurally safe and sound. Some assumed that, even when buildings were showing signs of instability, one had only to keep building until geometric regularity was achieved for all to be well. We take warning from William Golding's terrifying novel *The Spire*. Geometry was vital in any consideration of medieval sacred space, but it could also be dangerous!

This emphasis on geometry has a parallel in theological thinking. Medieval scholasticism led theologians to attempt to construct a framework or system of thought within which all positions on a particular issue of theology could be fitted together, so that they were logically consistent and reinforced one another. What theologians sought to do with religious treatises, builders then tried to do when they designed Gothic cathedrals. The High Gothic cathedral sought to embody the whole of Christian knowledge, theological, moral, natural and historical, with everything in its place.

For us today, the geometry and mathematical perfection of medieval buildings are hugely awe-inspiring (Illustration 2). 'How

Illustration 2

The perfection, elegance and symmetry of the Chapel of King's College
Cambridge, completed in 1547, still inspire and inform contemporary ideas
about the nature of God.

did they do it in those days?' is a frequently asked question in our
cathedrals. Indeed, the perfection, balance and proportion of the
finest of our cathedrals and sacred spaces may well speak to us about
God: these images of beauty, balance and proportion surely feed our
contemporary society with much-needed images of that God of

perfection. But, equally for us today, it is important to place into these perfect areas elements which help us see images of God that are not perfect. If God is to be made sense of amid the horrors of the twentieth century with its world wars and of the twenty-first century with its terrorism, then surely our sacred space must reflect this; otherwise, we will simply associate God with grandeur, perfection and inaccessibility. This is why contemporary art is so vital and why Hussey's work at Chichester was so essential and groundbreaking in the mid-twentieth century. Such art challenges and often shocks us into re-thinking our images of God. The conjunction of ancient and modern – of geometric perfection with the *avant garde* – is hugely powerful when we think of sacred space today.

The sacred space of Coventry Cathedral is made so much more powerful by the inclusion of elements which are the opposite of perfect and regular – for example the rough-hewn font made of a boulder from Bethlehem. Another example is 'Our Lady of Peace' at Tewkesbury Abbey,[1] where the fourteenth-century perfection of its sacred space is challenged by a contemporary image: in this case, the image of Our Lady, in stainless steel, rises serene out of a base of rusted metal – symbol of chaos (Illustration 3). Sacred space should produce awe and wonder, but it should also provoke thought, even disturbance, and should lead us to a more comprehensive portfolio of our images of God.

Sacred Space and Light

Light is a vital ingredient in any consideration of sacred space in medieval church buildings. In medieval theology, God concealed himself so as to be revealed, and light was the principal means by which humans could know him. One of the great sacred spaces of the medieval period is St Denis, which Abbot Suger based on the thought of Dionysius the Areopagite. At the heart of this theology was one central idea – God is light. Abbot Suger's church and indeed many other great medieval structures manifest this idea. Light had to

---

1   Our Lady of Peace, by Anthony Robinson (1991).

Illustration 3

Antony Robinson's 1991 statue of 'Our Lady of Peace' in Tewkesbury Abbey, standing in creative tension with its context. Photo by Tim Bridges.

penetrate into every corner of the interior space. This quest to achieve greater openings to admit more light necessitated the piercing of walls, bigger windows – anything that would admit more light to this image of the Heavenly Jerusalem.[2]

Often, however, light in a medieval church is effective because of its sheer paucity. The little Norman church of Heath Chapel, (Illustration 4) nestled against the Brown Clee in South Shropshire has nothing like the grandeur of light we associate with King's Chapel, but the darkness pierced by narrow shafts of light through tiny Norman windows gives a feeling of the numinous, which is just as potent. The Holy House at Walsingham is one the best examples where light is hugely effective because of the cavernous darkness. We should remember that when light did penetrate into our medieval churches, it often illuminated not plain limestone walls but a riot of colour and scenes both very beautiful and very frightening. The Reformers smashed stained glass to allow in the pure light; and when it entered the buildings, it lit up not Popish and superstitious paintings, but plain walls or walls with biblical texts. To the Reformers, light was needed not to illuminate the Heavenly Jerusalem within, but to throw light on the pure Word of God.

One of the great challenges for those of us who care for churches today is how we should reinforce sacred space through artificial light. In the contemporary world where, through the theatre and the media, we are so conscious of the power of lighting, a church can often fail to make the most of its sacred space by inappropriate lighting. The sense of the numinous is utterly compromised by poor, inadequate lighting. One manifestation of light which is found in both medieval and modern sacred space is, of course, the candle – that potent symbol of light in darkness which finds such a vital place in the spirituality of so many. For them, their experience of light through the candle transforms a visit to sacred space, whether it be at the Holy House or in the churches and cathedrals of our land.

---

2   Other examples of churches where light floods sacred space: King's College, Cambridge; Blythburgh and Donnington in Suffolk; and the lovely church at South Creake in Norfolk.

Illustration 4

Narrow shafts of light streaming through tiny windows pierce the darkness of
the little Norman church of Heath Chapel, nestled against the Brown Clee in
South Shropshire. Photo by Tim Bridges.

Sacred Space – Nothing but the Best!

To the medieval mind, sacred space had to be created and also built. The medieval worldview did not lend itself to the idea, present in other cultures, that natural places – caves, trees, forests – might be suitable settings for attracting the holy into their midst. Moreover, such spaces had to be built of substantial materials: stone was the ideal medium, since its strength and longevity communicate the unchanging nature of the sacred space. This bringing down of the divine into the midst of human beings suggests that whatever material might be used, nothing but the best is good enough.

It is worth noting the following exchange between Bernard of Clairvaux and Abbot Suger, where Bernard asks: 'What is the good of displaying all this gold in the church? . . . You display the statue of a saint . . . and you think that the more overloaded with colours it is, the holier it is . . . The church sparkles and gleams on all sides, while its poor huddle in need; its stones are gilded while its children go unclad; in it the art lovers find enough to satisfy their curiosity, while the poor find nothing there to relieve their misery.'[3] Suger replies: 'We maintain that the sacred vessels should be enhanced by outward adornment, and nowhere more than in serving the Holy Sacrifice, where inwardly all should be pure and outwardly all should be noble.'[4] Of course, this is an argument, elaboration or not, which has raged since the time of Christ, and earlier than that. 'You have the poor with you always . . .'[5]

The insistence on 'nothing but the best' when it comes to sacred space is most movingly seen in windows and carvings which are impossible to view from ground level – sections of stonework which are back-carved. Look at this picture of a roof boss in the Lady Chapel at Hereford (Illustration 5). I took this when scaffolding was in place and I could touch the boss. But from the floor it can hardly

---

3 Quoted in G. Duby, *The Age of the Cathedrals*, English translation of *Le temps des cathe-drals* (London, 1981), pp. 122–3.
4 Ibid., p. 98.
5 Matthew 26.11.

Illustration 5

A roof-boss in the Lady Chapel at Hereford Cathedral. The head of Christ is shown rising triumphantly above three entwining dragons, details that would always have been invisible from floor-level. Photo by Michael Tavinor.

be seen, certainly not so as to distinguish the detail – the head of Christ surrounded by entwining dragons, no doubt an image of the resurrection and of Christ triumphing over death. Sacred space is to celebrate God first and foremost and only then to provide nourishment for the worshipper.

And what of today? We would certainly not want to limit the influence of the sacred to built space. Our spirituality has to embrace the sacred space at the roadside shrine, the site of a road accident; our sacred space has to include the shrine of flowers at the gates of Kensington Palace or at Stockwell tube station or at Hillsborough stadium. Recent legislation challenges us to find sacred space outside the church, whether it be weddings in the ballroom of a hotel or in an air-balloon, or funerals in a woodland burial site.

Sacred Space and a Sense of Mystery

Medieval churches did not enable a worshipper or pilgrim to see the full sacredness of the place all at once. Cathedrals were divided into spaces of more concentrated sacredness as one progressed. This sense of mystery was enhanced by many means. Steps provided a major sense of mystery in Canterbury Cathedral, where there are 38 steps from the floor of the Nave to the site of Becket's shrine, resulting in a difference of 25 feet from one plane to the other. Screens were powerful in enhancing this sense of mystery: look at examples throughout Devon, or at one of the great screens of the Welsh borders such as St Margaret's in Herefordshire, or Patricio in the hills above Abergavenny. In all these buildings, screens beckon us on to glimpse the sacred beyond.

This sense of mystery is emphasized by allowing only certain people to experience the sacred. In Ely in 1300, the Bishop issued a statute banning female access to the Cathedral Choir where Etheldreda's shrine stood, at least on certain occasions. A marble line set in the floor at the west end of Durham Cathedral speaks of inclusion and exclusion in sacred space. Such a feeling was also heightened by the use of Latin and by the use of incense – both contributing to the sense of entering the sacred, the special, the mysterious.

We need to sense also the 'walled-in' feeling of the inner sanctuary surrounded by ambulatories and exterior walls. These in turn were encased by a Cathedral Close. Some cathedrals enhanced this sense of mystery by having worship conducted from high level – witness the singing gallery high on the north side of the Nave at Exeter Cathedral and the amazing west front at Wells Cathedral, with its gallery inside, and holes opening to the west front, through which choristers and clergy sang. This was sacred space being projected into the outside world. This was sacred space drawing one upwards – not only through sight but also through hearing.

Some sacred spaces were designed to transport you, mystically, into other sacred spaces: round churches (the Temple Church in London or the Round Church in Cambridge) remind us of the Holy Sepulchre in Jerusalem; the Holy House at Walsingham transports us to the Holy House of Nazareth. Pilgrims may not be able to get to the actual shrines themselves, but in prayer and imagination they can still enjoy its benefits and sense its holiness. Nor was this sense of 'sacred space by proxy' limited to the Catholic world: when chapels in Wales were named 'Bethel' and 'Ebenezer' and 'Horeb', worshippers were encouraged to see themselves as inhabiting these holy places. One aim of sacred space was to evoke surprise, astonishment, wonder and awe.

Ideas of sacred space and mystery change. Screens were often banished in the early nineteenth century, as people warmed to the romantic notion of the panoramic view. Nowadays we can see from one end of the cathedral to the other at Peterborough, at Southwark and at Salisbury. In the cases where screens were restored by Sir George Gilbert Scott, their function is largely cosmetic, as at Worcester, Lichfield or Durham – and the same applies to the screen that was removed at Hereford.

Perhaps, however, we are regaining this medieval idea of not revealing all of the holy at once. The arrangement of the newly restored Portsmouth Cathedral is a case in point: there, in the liturgy, we move from Nave to the place of baptism, on into the Choir for gathered worship and then on to the east end, the place of reservation of the Blessed Sacrament. Our sense of progression in sacred space is very much governed by the sense of progression in the liturgy itself. I, for one, simply cannot imagine that the Shrine Church at Walsingham would have a fraction of its mystery and wonder were all the chapel walls and screens to be removed and we were to be left with one large open-plan building. At a stroke, it would lose that atmosphere of mystery and wonder – that sense of wonder I feel as I move from chapel to chapel and, most wonderful of all, ascend those steps to the Chapel of the Assumption, with the Blessed Sacrament.

Sacred Space and its Protection

In the medieval building, sacredness was there, through mystery and light and geometry, but it needed to be 'topped up'. This was done through the liturgy and, not least, through processions. These ceremonies renewed and strengthened the line between the sacred and the profane. The most important focuses in the liturgy were marked in some of the 'Old Foundation' cathedrals with stones in the floor marking places where the principal persons in the liturgy stood. These stones were there to mark out sacred space. These sacred markers are still created. I actually had one of these placed in the floor at Tewkesbury Abbey, in the centre of the Nave; it was a slate roundel for the millennium, marked with MM and the inscription *locus evangelisti,* the place where the deacon reads the gospel at High Mass. No doubt I shall be reviled by my successors for having cast in stone – literally – a liturgical practice of the late twentieth century!

Since medieval times views have varied as to how much protection needed to be provided for sacred space. Archbishop Laud had definite views: his statute commanded the use of altar rails guarding the sanctuary. Laudian period altar rails may be found at the Saxon church at Deerhurst and at the 1662 church at Monnington-on-Wye near Hereford. Other periods have been cavalier in the extreme. Cartoons in *The Reformation and the Deformation,* published by Mowbray in 1868, give a wonderful picture of neglect in a sacred space – a mean table in the sanctuary, covered with the hats and coats of the parson and parishioners.

And what of protecting sacred space today? Sometimes if it is protected, it is by ropes and chrome pillars and notices saying 'No entry', or 'Evensong is about to begin, will visitors please leave the building'. A predecessor of mine as vicar of Tewkesbury Abbey, Canon Ernest Smith, had definite ideas about the way in which sacred space was compromised by the newly arrived day-trippers from Birmingham. He wrote in the parish magazine for 1924:

> No one knows as well as our Sacristan the utter lack of reverence shown by the average 'tripper': left to wander at their own sweet will, these 'trippers' would (as they often do) behave themselves unseemly, and do irreparable damage to the monuments, etc. The fact is, the English lower middle class have very little appreciation of the unique and priceless glories of such a building and still less conception of what a House of God is ... I myself deplore that necessity for a fee as much as anyone, but until our 'trippers' are all Christians in fact as well as in name, there is, I fear, no practical alternative ...[6]

Canon Smith would not be a welcome member of the Heart of England Tourist Board; but he does raise some interesting contemporary questions about how we present the sacred to visitors who may well have no idea what it's all about.

This clash of cultures and the sacredness of a place being compromised by other factors are highlighted by the current discussion about whether or not to charge for entrance to our cathedrals. Not that this is a new idea – even though people speak of it as if it were. They started charging for entrance to the Royal Chapels at Westminster Abbey in 1820 and one of the first tasks of Dean Frank Bennett, when he became Dean of Chester in 1920, was to abolish charging. Nowadays, St Paul's, York and Ely charge and just recently Winchester has joined the band. Some deans are in favour, others not. Nicholas Frayling, Dean of Chichester, says that when cathedrals charge for entry, the experience is more like entering some exhibition or the Millennium Dome: it loses some of its spirituality.[7] Others claim the

---

6   *Tewkesbury Parochial Magazine*, July 1924, p. 91.
7   *Church Times*, 24 February 2006, p. 7.

contrary: that through paying, one may value the experience more, stay longer, find out more.

Sacred space does not remain static over periods of time. Each generation uses it in a different way. Consider the interior of Tewkesbury Abbey in 1820: the Nave was never used for worship, but for the burial of townsfolk. In the chancel, there was a central pulpit – a triple decker – with a tiny communion table at the east end and seats facing away from the table. How different is the scene 150 years later: the massive medieval stone *mensa* has been restored, six candles placed on the altar, the choir stalls restored and the clutter banished.

Each generation must interpret the sacredness. This may mean adding beautiful things – glass, icons, statues and contemporary art. It may also mean taking things away to enhance the sacredness – and, of course, this is a much more difficult process as any who have tried to remove a pew or other historical artefact know all too well. Colin Stephenson in his book *Walsingham Way*, describes the outcry in the shrine church when he tried to ease out some of the myriad reliquaries placed there by Fr Hope Patten.[8] The conservation lobby is often unhelpful, while ideas of the sacred and what would enhance it do not always fit in with current government or diocesan policy about the care of ancient churches.

Sacred Space and Pilgrimage

Sacred space in medieval times developed for all sorts of reasons. Some buildings were political expressions, others were built to glorify a family or dynasty. Thus Tewkesbury Abbey, sometimes known as the 'Westminster Abbey of the feudal baronage', is full of the tombs of the de Clares, the Despensers, the Beauchamps. Pilgrimage was far from the minds of those who built this church; indeed, having unwashed pilgrims in what amounted to their private mausoleum would have been far from their intentions.

Let us consider two examples of sacred spaces that developed as a result of pilgrimage. First, Canterbury Cathedral. After his martyrdom,

---

8   C. Stephenson, *Walsingham Way* (London, 1970).

Becket's body remained in the Crypt – there was no room for a shrine in the traditional place behind the high altar, even had the monks wanted one. However, the disastrous fire of 1171 gave opportunity for the rebuilding of the cathedral choir, and the provision of the most magnificent setting for any shrine in England. The Trinity Chapel, that great, expansive, horse-shoe-shaped apse, became the site of Becket's spectacular shrine, and this in turn led to the Corona, the eastern rotunda, in which was displayed the relic of Becket's scalp. The Trinity Chapel is the culmination of a series of rising floor levels. Here, seemingly, there was planned a deliberately theatrical presentation of the saint. Pilgrimage has had a huge influence on sacred space.

Secondly, Hereford Cathedral, which does not boast a martyr but does possess one of the few remaining shrine bases in its original position – that of Thomas Cantilupe, who died in 1282 and whose cult at one stage rivalled that of Becket in numbers of pilgrims and miracles. The shape of Hereford Cathedral was greatly influenced by this saint's cult, not least in the rebuilding of the central tower through the generous gifts of pilgrims – the tower even now adorned with elaborate ball-flower decoration. But it was the new processional ways that lent special drama and sacred space to the cult of Cantilupe, who was canonized in 1320. The canonization gave an opportunity to exult the office of bishop and to proclaim to all who came to Hereford as pilgrims that one of this glorious company had 'made it' to the order of sainthood. On each side of the Quire are the choir aisles, and each choir aisle is lined with the tombs of the bishops who followed Cantilupe. Pilgrims would have passed these tombs en route to the shrine of the sainted bishop.

Sacred Space and Memory

The great minds of the ancient and medieval worlds were, it seems, able to learn huge tracts of the written word by heart; there was a need to remember texts, arguments and lessons. Paper was scarce and so memory was vital. It seems that features of cathedrals were used as 'icons' or 'reminders' which would open up to the rememberer whole areas of the Bible and the Fathers. Today, however, we think in the visual and remember in the visual; but cathedrals and sacred spaces can still put over the Christian message in exciting and memorable ways. Vast space, colour, sound, light, music: these can speak of the Christian message more powerfully than the word alone.

There are two practical points to be borne in mind. First, the presentation of sacred space is vital. We totally underestimate the 'turn-off' effect of dirt and lack of care in our sacred spaces. Nothing can ever totally take away the feeling of awe that we experience in the great French cathedrals; but how much more profound would be this awe if they were cared for, if there were not stacks of chairs all over the place and half-dead poinsettias on no longer used side altars. Sacred space so often needs to be just that – space, with nothing in it. So often, alas, our nerve fails: in sneaks unwanted furniture that we thought we had banished.

Secondly, even before we enter sacred space, we can be made ready to experience it. I can count on the fingers of one hand the church notice-boards I have seen recently that are really well kept, informative and attractive. Careful presentation says to us, and to our visitors and pilgrims, that what we are entering is important. Sacred spaces are God-given, but they also rely on human beings to co-operate with God to present this sacred space in the most appropriate and beautiful way.

Sacred Space Defined by Contrast to Secular Space

We come now to a consideration of sacred space and its secular influences. Often sacred space has been defined as the opposite of secular space – the former as divine space, the latter as human space, both being kept in separate compartments. A brief look at history will enable us to see whether or not this really is the case. In the early Church, there seems to have been little evidence of this hard division: churches were used for living and sleeping, eating and drinking, for meetings and for legal proceedings. This conjunction continued in the Middle Ages. Churches were used for the distribution of poor relief, for the playing of games, for acting, teaching, dancing. There were library facilities in churches and church-towers were used for the defence of a village. And Paul's Walk within the Cathedral in London was a veritable market place! So, in medieval churches sacred space and secular space were often one and the same thing.

Alongside this, there developed a view that church space was very much sacred space: Leon Battista Alberti (1404–72) in his *De Re Aedificatoria Libri Decem*, insists that God's temples should not be profaned by any secular use: 'As there is nothing in nature can be imagined more holy or noble than our sacrifice, so I believe that no man of sense can be for having it debased by being made too common.'[9] Interestingly, Alberti calls his churches *Temples* and sees nothing wrong in using models from pagan Rome as prototypes of Christian buildings. This is in marked contrast to later generations and especially to the ideas of the Gothic Revival, which could not countenance the imitation of classical temples – they were seen as clear expressions of heathenism and could not possibly be a vehicle for sacred space.

In Baroque culture, sacred space is often linked with the theatre. Church is a place apart, yet it is greatly influenced in design by the opera. Churches have a proscenium arch. Often, the chief focus is no longer the Mass, but the exposition of the sacrament. 'In the presence of the Divine King, a kind of heavenly grand opera could be performed, with all the display of lights, jewels (mainly false), exquisite polyphonic singing and pageantry which commonly accompany a royal reception.'[10] Santa Maria della Salute in Venice is the supreme example: a round auditorium, looking onto a rectangular choir, which has all the feeling of a theatrical stage. Sacred and secular: the dividing lines are again blurred. Consider, too, the pilgrimage church of Weiss in southern Germany: the confection, seen in stonework and carving, could as well be in a theatre as in church.

What about Anglican worship? Wren was against the division of church buildings into chancel and nave and, by inference, against the

9   L. B. Alberti, *Ten Books on Architecture*, ed. and trans. J. Leoni (London, 1955), VII, I, p. 133.
10   L. Bouyer, *Life and Liturgy*. (London, 1956), p. 7.

different uses of nave and chancel, secular and sacred. He is quite clear what sacred space was for: 'The Romanists indeed may build larger churches, it is enough if they hear the Murmur of the Mass and see the elevation of the host, but ours are to be fitted for auditories.'[11] Also interesting is the rather muddled Puritan view of these things: on one hand, holy places were scriptural, with some relation to the Temple at Jerusalem; on the other, they were reminders of the hated popery. Anglican leaders were accused of: 'attributing special holiness to places and things by their appointment and consecrations: as if without their consecration all things were unclean, nothing fit for holy uses . . .'[12] And so, famously, Cromwell's soldiers stabled their horses in cathedrals and thought nothing of it.

Sacred space is a paradox, found in scripture, found in conflicting views throughout history and here articulated most clearly by the Quaker George Fox: 'The steeple-houses and pulpits were offensive to my mind, because both priests and people called them the House of God, and idolized them; reckoning that God dwelt there in the outward house. Whereas they should have looked for God and Christ to dwell in their hearts, and their bodies to be made temples of God; for the apostle said, God dwelleth not in temples made with hands.'[13] This simplicity is, perhaps, best represented by the many wonderful seventeenth-century Quaker meeting houses.

In the nineteenth century, with the Gothic Revival, this clear division of sacred and secular in sacred spaces became very marked. Renaissance architecture was seen as pagan. Church must be in Gothic style and divided into different rooms, corresponding with degrees of holiness. Pugin would have hated St Francis Xavier's in Hereford, dating from 1830, and based on the Treasury of the Athenians in Delphi. Pugin was clear: sacred space could never be found in buildings like that. The strict Anglican division of sacred and secular is nowhere better seen than in the erection of church

---

11 Christopher Wren, quoted by G. W. O. Addleshaw and F. Etchells, *The Architectural Setting of Anglican Worship*. (London, 1948), p. 249.
12 Quoted in *Hierurgia Anglicana* III, revised edn by V. Staley, (1904), p. 337.
13 *The Journal of George Fox* (8th edn, London, 1891), vol. I, p. 8.

halls from the end of the nineteenth century. By the second decade of the twentieth century, nearly every urban and suburban church had one. If the Christian community was to perform any social service requiring rooms, the accommodation had to be provided *outside* the liturgical area. We in the Church of England have taken a long time to free ourselves from this tyranny.

Another issue bearing on sacred space is the vexed one concerning pews. The early church did not have them, of course, while often medieval churches had only a stone bench. Until that period, sacred space had no connection with the degree of comfort associated with the home. Eventually, sacred and secular converged as churches in the course of the eighteenth century became extraordinarily comfortable, at least for the wealthy, including family pews, sofas, fireplaces and drinks cabinets. People were comfortable at home, so why not in church? The inhospitability of churches today is something the eighteenth century would not have subscribed to. So often today sacred space means discomfort: an austere form of devotion is imposed on all, if they are prepared to submit to it.

Are we right, then, to separate sacred and secular when it comes to sacred space? History suggests that the dividing lines are really quite blurred and that religious observance is often richer when there is a right understanding of ways in which sacred space embraces the secular. Indeed, one historian goes so far as to say: 'The final separation of churches for Church services alone, desired by all the greater and more pious men who have served them, has been accompanied by a reduction of the fulness of their strength and meaning.'[14]

Coda

My ending is with a Hereford image – that of the famous *Mappa Mundi*. It is dated to the end of the thirteenth century and, when new, was possibly associated with the shrine of St Thomas Cantilupe and intended to lure pilgrims into the building. In many respects, it

---

14   A. R. Powys, *The English Parish Church* (London, 1930), p. 164.

is not a geographical map at all, but a theological one. At the top of the map is an image of Christ in Glory, as if the image were saying: Christ in Majesty is king over the whole of creation. On this medieval map we will find *bona fide* holy places: the Holy Sepulchre at Jerusalem, St Peter's in Rome; we will find also places sacred in classical mythology: the labyrinth, the Parthenon; and we will find strange mythical creatures: the basilisk, the unicorn. There is no sacred and secular – all is sacred space, as Christ the King is Lord over it all.

Chapter 3

The Book as Sacred Space

Michelle P. Brown

Illuminated copies of scripture are a suitable, if initially somewhat surprising, subject for a discussion of sacred space. For they enable us to glimpse many ways in which our medieval forebears saw themselves in relation to time, to space and to the divine. They frequently occupied focal positions at the pilgrimage centres of their day, serving as a visible focus of devotion and contemplation at the shrines of usually invisible saints (unless of course we are talking about venerable figures such as St Bishoi, in the Egyptian Wadi Natroun, whom pilgrims can still prod to ensure that he is enduring, incorrupt, inside his vestments). Another of the miraculously incorrupt saints of the early Middle Ages was, of course, St Cuthbert, who was commemorated by his community's great 'book of the high altar', the Lindisfarne Gospels.[1]

The decorated incipit to St John's Gospel in the Lindisfarne Gospels[2] (see Illustration 6), probably conceived and made by Bishop Eadfrith of Lindisfarne on Holy Island around 710–720, reminds us immediately of the underlying basis of the medieval approach to

---

1   For a full discussion of the Lindisfarne Gospels (British Library, Cotton MS Nero D.iv) and of the issues in relation to it discussed here, see M. P. Brown, *The Lindisfarne Gospels: Society, Spirituality and the Scribe* (Luzern, London and Toronto, 2003); see also M. P. Brown, '"In the Beginning was the Word": Books and Faith in the Age of Bede', *Jarrow Lecture* (2000). For an introduction to Insular and Anglo-Saxon manuscripts in general, see M. P. Brown, *Manuscripts from the Anglo-Saxon Age* (London and Toronto, 2006). For their context, see, for example, M. P. Brown, *How Christianity Came to Britain and Ireland* (Oxford, 2006).

2   British Library, Cotton MS Nero D.iv, f. 211r.

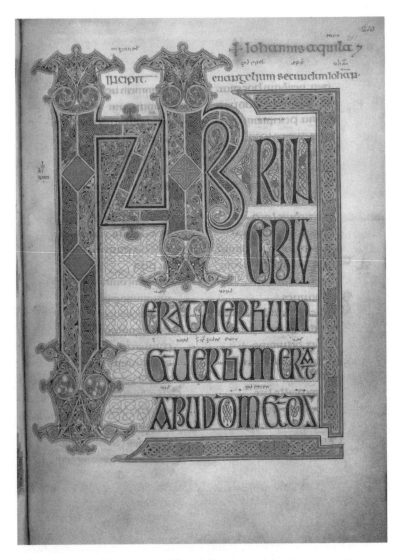

Illustration 6

The decorated incipit to St John's Gospel in the Lindisfarne Gospels,
which were probably made on Holy Island around 710–720.

sacred text by elevating to due prominence the opening words of what Bede described as 'the little Gospel that treats of the things that work of love': 'In the beginning was the Word, and the Word was with God, and the Word was God' (John 1.1). *Logos*, the Word, was the very embodiment of the Creator, revealed to Creation through the incarnation, death and resurrection of Christ and through the abiding physical manifestation of the gospel book that contained his teachings, itself incarnated through the combination of divine inspiration, the quickening of human labour and the materials – animal, plant and mineral – of Creation. That book became, literally, the Word made flesh, or rather, the Word made word.

Hebrew scribes had adopted the practice of according particular veneration to the *nomina sacra*, the sacred names by which the Lord was known, by writing them in abbreviated form as sacred symbols, a practice that Christians extended to their early copies of scripture; the *chi-rho* – the first letters of 'Christus' in Greek – becoming a particularly potent early Christian device. When the *chi-rhos* in books such as the Lindisfarne Gospels[3] (see Illustration 7) and the Book of Kells explode across the page, they become icons in their own right and may perhaps have helped to allay concerns over iconoclasm at a time when the problem of idolatry was actively discussed in Judaic, Islamic and Christian circles. The debate resurfaced throughout the early Middle Ages and was hotly contested in the west, despite the teaching of Gregory the Great, in a letter addressed *c.*600 to Bishop Serenus of Marseilles, that 'in images the illiterate read'. Nonetheless, early medieval copies of Christian scripture are amongst the most beautiful examples of the illuminator's art, their precious contents often enshrined within similarly precious covers – an acknowledgement of their symbolic power at a time when, at the height of eastern iconoclasm, only the Cross and the Book were acceptable visual symbols of faith and the spatial foci of veneration and of gatherings for worship.

We are familiar with the medieval Islamic concept of sacred calligraphy – the beautification of the Word serving as a means of praising

---

3   British Library, Cotton MS Nero D.iv, f. 18r.

Illustration 7

A decorated Chi-Rho page from the Lindisfarne Gospels, introducing the
Nativity narrative in St Matthew's Gospel. It features the massive 'Chi-rho'
symbol, formed from the initial letters of Christos and providing a powerful
icon in a period when actual representations were still provoking controversy.

the divine – and I suggest that this idea first found full expression amongst the monastic artist-scribes of Britain and Ireland during the seventh and eighth centuries. Byzantium, ever concerned to contain the schisms that endangered its hegemony, led the way in the debate. Byzantine book production had flourished during the early Christian period, readily embracing imagery (although little now survives), but hit an all-time low during the Iconoclast Controversy (720s to 787). Imagery was largely outlawed, with only the book and the cross being considered acceptable public manifestations of belief and art. With the Council of Nicaea (787) and the accession of Empress Irene (797–802) images were reinstated and, despite an iconoclastic resurgence in 814–843, book production was stepped up again within the Byzantine Empire.[4]

The Carolingian stance on imagery, in which scholars such as Alcuin of York participated, was controversial. They used it to emphasize the interdependence of Church and State – the emperor combining the symbolic roles of king and priest – but remained troubled by idolatry. The Carolingian response to the Council of Nicaea took the form of the *Libri Carolini* by Theodulf of Orléans, in which the primacy of the word was asserted over images, which were permitted but deemed to possess no inherent holiness or iconic value.[5] Copies of scripture produced from this time until *c*.810 (when the Lorsch Gospels once more dared depict Christ in Majesty) are noticeably devoid of pictures of the divine, preferring illustrations of biblical narratives or evangelist portraits. This of course made way, conveniently, for the development of royal iconography.[6]

4   See E. Kitzinger, *The Place of Book Illumination in Byzantine Art* (Princeton, 1975); D. Buckton, ed., *Byzantium: Treasures of Byzantine Art and Culture* (London, 1994); J. Lowden, *Early Christian and Byzantine Art* (London, 1997); L. Safran, ed., *Heaven on Earth: Art and the Church in Byzantium* (University Park, PA, 1998).
5   W. Diebold, *Word and Image: A History of Early Medieval Art* (Boulder, 2000), pp. 100–1, 117–18.
6   F. Mütherich, F. and J. Gaehde, *Carolingian Painting* (London, 1976); for aspects of ruler imagery, see R. Deshman, 'The Exalted Servant: The Ruler Theology of the Prayer-book of Charles the Bald', *Viator* 11 (1980), pp. 385–417 and P. Dutton and H. Kessler, *The Poetry and Painting of the First Bible of Charles the Bald* (Ann Arbor, 1997).

So, from the very beginnings of the rise of the codex (book) form, first popularized by its use for containing Christian scripture, was itself a sacred space – a tabernacle of the Word and a place for the enshrinement and contemplation of ideals. This space could be inhabited both by the maker and the viewer. For those who dedicated their lives to God's service, to be entrusted with the transmission of his Word, as preachers and as scribes, was a high calling indeed. In a letter to Bishop Acca of Hexham concerning his commentary on Luke, Bede wrote 'I have subjected myself to that burden of work in which, as in innumerable bonds of monastic servitude which I shall pass over, I was myself at once author, notary, and scribe'.[7] This revealing passage shows that he regarded such work as an act of *opus dei*, and that he differentiated between the functions of author, secretary and scriptural transmitter.

Cassiodorus, in his *Institutiones*, said that each word written was 'a wound on Satan's body', assigning the scribe the role of *miles Christi* (soldier of Christ). In the same work he says that in those who translate, expand or humbly copy scripture the Spirit continues to work, as in the biblical authors who were first inspired to write them. Scripture lends the scribal analogy to the Lord himself (see Jeremiah 31.33; Hebrews 10.16; Ps. 44/45.1–2). Cassiodorus also advocated (in the *Institutiones* and his *Commentary* on Psalm 44/45.1–2) that the scribe could preach with the hand and 'unleash tongues with the fingers', imitating the action of the Lord who wrote the Law with his all-powerful finger.[8] Bede pursued this theme in relation to Ezra the Scribe, who fulfilled the Law by restoring its destroyed books, dictating them from memory and thereby opening his mouth to interpret

---

7   D. Hurst, ed., *Bede, Expositio in Lucam*, Corpus Christianorum, Series Latina 120 (1960), prol. 93–115; M. Stansbury, 'Early Medieval Biblical Commentaries, Their Writers and Readers', in K. Hauck, ed., *Frümittelalterliche Studien, Herausgegeben von H. Keller und C. Meier* (Berlin and New York, 1999), pp. 50–82, at p. 72.

8   Cassiodorus, *De Institutione Divinarum Litterarum*, ch. 30; see *Magni Aurelii*, Corpus Christianorum, Series Latina 96; Migne, *Patrologiae Cursus Completus* 70 (Paris, 1847), cols 1144–5. See also J. O'Reilly, 'The Library of Scripture: Views from the Vivarium and Wearmouth-Jarrow', in P. Binski and W. G. Noel, eds, *New Offerings, Ancient Treasures: Essays in Medieval Art for George Henderson* (Stroud, 2001) and Brown, *Lindisfarne Gospels*, ch. 5.

scripture and teach others. The act of writing is therefore presented as an essential act for the preacher-teacher-scribe.[9]

Such exhortations may have influenced the production of the Lindisfarne Gospels, for this remarkable book is the work of a single artist-scribe.[10] Some modern scribes estimate that at least two years of full-time work in optimum conditions would be required to make it.[11] Although contemporary Ethiopian scribes in the South Gondar region, employing much the same methods and materials as when Christianity became their state religion during the fourth century, can write an undecorated religious codex of some 400 leaves in around eight to twelve months. They write for two or three hours per day amidst agricultural and church duties, simply resting the leaves on their knees as they squat on the ground to write.[12] Undertaking such an heroic feat of patience alongside the monastic duties of the Divine Office (celebrated eight times each day and night), prayer, study and manual labour, suggests that making the Lindisfarne Gospels may have taken closer to five years, depending on how much exemption was granted from other duties, such as that accorded to anchorites. If, as seems likely, Bishop Eadfrith of Lindisfarne (698–721) both conceived the vision for its gospelbook and physically made it himself, his responsibility for the largest dioceses in Britain would have made such work additionally challenging and difficult to focus on. Some of it was probably undertaken on Cuddy's Isle, a windswept tidal islet in the bay beside the monastery on Holy Island, where for the seasons of Lent and Advent the bishop retired on retreat – a watery wilderness in which the hermit was emptied out, to be filled with the Spirit and the energy to recommit.

Such solitary eremitic scribal labour may have been a distinctive 'Celtic' approach to work as living prayer.[13] For whereas the copying

---

9   See O'Reilly, 'The Library of Scripture'.
10   Brown, *Lindisfarne Gospels.*
11   I have spoken to a number of contemporary scribes on this matter, including some of the team currently working with Donald Jackson on a complete hand-produced Bible for the Benedictine monastery of St John's, Collegeville, Minnesota.
12   J. Mellors and A. Parsons, *Ethiopian Bookmaking* and *Scribes of South Gondar* (London, 2002).
13   Brown, 'In the Beginning was the Word' and *Lindisfarne Gospels.*

of other texts was the cenobitic work of the scriptorium, transmitting scripture was entrusted only to the senior members of the community. Within the Columban tradition saints Canice and Columba were acclaimed as hero-scribes,[14] for in copying the gospels the scribe became an evangelist in turn and, by study, contemplation and meditation upon the text (*ruminatio, contemplatio* and *meditatio*), might actually glimpse the divine (*revelatio*). This accorded with the patristic concept of the 'inner library' in which each believer became a library of the divine Word, a sacred responsibility which the Irish sage Cummian referred to as 'entering the Sanctuary of God' by studying and transmitting scripture.[15] Books became the vessels from which the believer's inner ark was filled – enablers of direct Christian action, channels of the Spirit, and gateways to revelation. Such books are portals of prayer. Just as St Cuthbert struggled with his demons on the rock of his Inner Farne hermitage on behalf of all, so the bishop-monk who produced the Lindisfarne Gospels as Cuthbert's cult-book undertook an heroic feat of patience and of spiritual and physical endurance – part of the apostolic mission of bringing the Word of God to the furthest reaches of the known world, enshrining it there within the new Temple of the Word, the Book.

As with many other aspects of Celtic eremitic monasticism inherited from the east, the communities producing such books may have reflected the practices of the semi-eremitic *lavras* of the Syro-Palestinian monastic tradition, where monks came together for communal worship but lived separately as quasi-anchorites. The gospel book became the scribal desert and via the 'desert' islands of Britain and Ireland, influences from the Middle East, the cradle of the biblical tradition, were transmitted to the west alongside the latinized, imperial influences of Rome and a pre-Christian appreciation of Nature as what St Columbanus termed a second scripture.

---

14   Brown, 'In the Beginning was the Word' and *Lindisfarne Gospels*; R. G. Gameson, 'The Scribe Speaks? Colophons in Early English Manuscripts', *H. M. Chadwick Memorial Lectures* 12 (2001).
15   See M. Walsh and D. Ó Cróinín, eds, *Cummian's Letter De Controversia Paschale*, (Toronto, 1988), pp. 15–18, 57–9. See O'Reilly, 'The Library of Scripture'.

The balancing of approaches, from the temporal territories of east and west, was undertaken in the Insular gospel books with remarkable sensitivity, their conflation of cultural references reflecting the counterpoint of the exegetical writings of figures such as Gregory the Great and Bede. Unity and the avoidance of schism were major considerations, apparent in the careful balancing of iconic and aniconic features at a time when iconoclasm was rife. Its evangelist miniatures sit like framed icons on the page, set against polished pink grounds intended to recall encaustic icons painted with wax. They portray aspects of Christ's nature obliquely through their symbolism – the evangelist symbols providing a visual exegesis upon aspects of the nature of Christ: Matthew, the man of the incarnation; Mark the lion of kingship and resurrection; Luke the calf or bull, the sacrificial offering; and John, the eagle of the second coming, who soars directly to the throne of God for inspiration.[16]

Early Church Councils spent much time debating the nature of Christ and the question of how he embodied the reconciliation of the human and the divine. The crucial Council of Chalcedon (451), however, pronounced that Christ possessed two natures, human and divine, which co-existed but were not commingled. The Egyptians objected, championing the Monophysite belief that he possessed only one nature, causing a breach between the Orthodox and Monophysite (West Syriac or Jacobite, Coptic and Ethiopic) Churches.[17] This made the subject of the Virgin and her relationship to Christ a particular source of interest and may have shaped early medieval responses to depictions of the Virgin and Child. The Copts were keen to stress the maternal relationship and their approach seems to have influenced that of Insular artists, who were amongst the earliest in the west to illustrate the Virgin with the Christ-child on her knee. Such images appear on the coffin of St Cuthbert, around 700, and in the Book of Kells, around 800, and were probably derived from Coptic adaptations of the iconography from ancient Egyptian effigies of Isis and Horus.

---

16 See the St John miniature, in the Lindisfarne Gospels, British Library, Cotton MS Nero D.iv, f. 209v.

17 F. Déroche and F. Richard, *Scribes et manuscrits du Moyen-Orient* (Paris, 1997).

Such matters also have a bearing on how Eadfrith chose to depict the evangelists in relation to time and space. Two of the Lindisfarne Gospels' evangelists are bearded and ageing, two are youthful and immortal. This is not, as some art historians have suggested, simply a response to the availability of different models – the former from Byzantium and the latter from Rome – but a subtle means of highlighting the complementary nature of the human and perishable and the divine and eternal, brought together in the unity of the Gospels in the one book and in Christ himself. Like their Byzantine counterparts, these Insular evangelists dwell within the abstract, timeless space of the icon, whether on painted or gilded grounds.

Like many other early gospel books, the Lindisfarne Gospels includes a set of canon tables within its prefatory matter (see Illustration 8).[18] Canon tables had been devised by Constantine's 'court bishop' Eusebius of Caesarea (died 338/339) as a concordance system in which the gospels were divided into numbered sections with parallel readings, all displayed in tabular form. Carl Nordenfalk has explored Eusebius's intention that the gospel harmony embodied in his canon tables should be 'a full epitome of the Holy Writ' and that 'in that capacity the Canon Tables partook in the sacredness of the Holy Word which they prefaced, and made them entitled to an unusually splendid adornment of their setting that pleases the eye and more than anything else accounts for the wide distribution of Eusebius' invention and the tenacity with which it survived.'[19] They are often set within arcades, with architectural columns sometimes painted to give the illusion of marble, sometimes filled with interlace or other decorative motifs, forming 'an impressive atrium at the entrance of the sacred text itself' – an invitation and means of entering the Holy of Holies through a numeric encapsulation of Christ's ministry.[20] One set of Insular canon tables, opening a gospel book now in St Petersburg (the St Petersburg Gospels, St Petersburg, State Library, MS Cod. F.v.I.8) which was probably made in Mercia during the second half of the

---

18   British Library, Cotton MS Nero D. iv, f. 17v.
19   C. Nordenfalk, *Studies in the History of Book Illumination* (London, 1992), p. 16.
20   Ibid., pp. 30 and 18; Brown, *The Lindisfarne Gospels*, ch. 5.

Illustration 8

Canon tables from the Lindisfarne Gospels, included within its introductory matter. They provide a concordance system for the Gospels, set within an architectural frame and providing a gateway into the texts themselves.

eighth century,[21] is very distinctive in its architectural form, featuring Islamic-style arches that may be intended to recall exotic features of the sort seen by northern European pilgrims, many of whom are known to have travelled to the holy places of the Middle East.

In the Lindisfarne Gospels, each major text is spatially distinguished from the others and introduced by exquisite cross carpet-pages, indebted to Coptic art and recalling in details of their decoration the *Crux Gemmata* (the jewelled cross, symbol of the Second Coming) and the prayer mats sometimes used in northern Europe at this time as well as in the Middle East (see Illustration 9: St John carpet-page[22]) – part of a shared ritual tradition in the Abrahamic religions that first emerged there.[23] For there is evidence of the currency of an *Ordo* at Wearmouth-Jarrow, with which Lindisfarne enjoyed a fruitful collaboration during the early eighth century that included the use of prayer mats during the Good Friday veneration of the Cross. The Lindisfarne Gospels' carpet pages may therefore prepare the entry onto the holy ground of sacred text, like actual prayer rugs, whilst the facing Incipits pay visual honour to the Word. Each of the five cross-carpet pages in the Lindisfarne Gospels features a different form of cross: Latin, Greek and other local forms. It may be that Eadfrith intended this as a symbolic celebration of regional diversity harmonized across space in ecumenical unity within the Book, reinforcing his subtle blending of diverse cultural influences to form an integrated, synthesized style of illumination that epitomized cultural interaction within an ecumen that stretched from the deserts of Palestine and Syria to the rocky outcrops of the Atlantic seaboard.

Another feature shared by both eastern and western Churches was the practice of enshrining sacred texts within the covers of precious treasure bindings, adorned with gold and silver, jewels, ivories or enamels. This made them equally powerful symbols of faith when closed, seen carried during liturgical procession, for example. Some books, which acquired the status of relics by virtue of their

---

21   See Brown, *Manuscripts from the Anglo-Saxon Age.*

22   British Library, Cotton MS Nero D iv, f. 210v.

23   Brown, *Lindisfarne Gospels.*

Illustration 9

A cross carpet-page from the Lindisfarne Gospels. Five such carpet-pages,
each consisting of a cross embedded in ornament resembling an eastern
prayer-mat, are distributed through the manuscript and provide another form
of introduction to those entering the sacred space of the Gospel texts.

association with a saint, might also be encased within reliquaries. One such was a book shrine made in Ireland during the late eighth century and cast into Lough Kinale when a disgruntled ninth-century Viking raider found that all it contained was an old book (the Lough Kinale Shrine is in the National Museum of Ireland, Dublin). Some such book-shrines were not made to be opened, indicating that it was the symbolic presence of the book within that was important.

Another good illustration of this mindset is the inclusion of a little copy of St John's Gospel within the coffin of Cuthbert – a theca, a container etymologically related to the bibliotheca itself – discovered within it by Bishop Flambard at the dedication of the Norman cathedral in 1104 and perhaps placed there at the translation of St Cuthbert's relics to the high altar at Lindisfarne in 698. This moving little volume, perhaps intended to recall Cuthbert's studies of St John's Gospel with his master Boisil at Melrose, had been written at Wearmouth-Jarrow and bound there in Coptic sewing fashion. It brings to mind another early example of the inclusion of a book in a Christian burial. The earliest extant Coptic Psalter[24] was excavated in a humble cemetery at Al-Mudil, some 40 km from Oxyrhynchus, where, around 400, it had lovingly been placed, open, as a pillow-book beneath the head of a young teenage girl. Its binding incorporates a key, shaped like the Egyptian cross-key of life, reinforcing the probability that this was an appropriation by the early Christian Copts of the ancient Egyptian practice of burying their deceased with a Book of the Dead to aid their passage into eternity. Placed within Cuthbert's coffin, the beautifully penned and bound copy of St John's Gospel likewise probably served an invisible sacral and talismanic function, sanctifying the sacred space inhabited by the saint's incorrupt body and guiding him on his journey, just as readings from John were used in ministrations to the sick and the dead.

A Carolingian gospel book in the British Library,[25] made at Tours

---

24   Cairo, The Coptic Museum, MSS. Library, 6614; see M. P. Brown, ed., *In the Beginning: Bibles Before the Year 1000* (Washington, 2006).
25   British Library, Add. MS 11848.

in the first half of the ninth century, is adorned with a splendid treasure binding that was undoubtedly made to be seen, featuring Christ enthroned at the Last Judgement. Within the thickness of its wooden boards it contains actual relic-bones of the saints, making it literally a reliquary and allowing it to serve as an altar which would also have contained relics. There is evidence of a number of important early gospel books serving as 'books of the high altar', often kept chained there (as the Lindisfarne Gospels probably were at Durham), where they served as visible symbols of their church's authority and that of its saint, and affirmed the sacrality of their most holy place – the high altar. Such was the impact and power of the written word of sacred text amongst the newly converted peoples of northern Europe that it helped to transform their societies and legal practices. One of St Augustine's first tasks upon leading his mission from Rome into Kent in 597 was to commit the lawcode of King Ethelberht to the 'safe-keeping of writing', allegedly inventing written Old English in the process and serving to legitimize his rule and to integrate the Church into the social structure. For this was a time when radical Christian teaching demonstrated its power to transform, causing seasoned warriors, raised on the *Beowulf*-like epics of the mead hall, to embrace pacifism and causing kings to free slaves, thereby threatening to overturn the social order. Within the Insular world the most solemn oaths and most important and binding legal transactions would therefore be solemnized and witnessed, before God and mortals alike, on the sacred ground of the 'book of the high altar'. We still swear our oaths upon sacred texts, or their secular substitutes. One of the earliest examples of this practice can be found in the St Chad Gospels,[26] made in the mid-eighth century and containing work by an artist who had studied the Lindisfarne Gospels in detail. In the mid-ninth century this volume was traded by a Welshman, Gelhi, for his best horse and presented by him to the altar of St Teilo at Llandeilo Fawr in Carmathenshire. There it was used, for a century, as a book of the high altar and contains records of oaths, property transfers and what may be the oldest document freeing

---

26   Lichfield Cathedral, MS 1.

slaves in the post-Roman world, some of them forming the oldest extant examples of written Welsh.

Another such was B.L. Royal MS 1.B.vii, an eighth-century Northumbrian gospel book which contains a manumission of slaves by King Athelstan, celebrating his accession in 924. The Coronation Gospels, a little Carolingian gospel book also associated with the ownership of Athelstan, an inveterate bibliophile and collector of relics, is identified by tradition (or at least a tradition identified by Sir Robert Cotton in the early seventeenth century) as the book upon which the early rulers of England swore their coronation oaths, just as the St Augustine Gospels, thought to have accompanied his mission from Rome, is still used at the installation of the Archbishop of Canterbury.[27]

Another, later medieval form of depicting sacred space in manuscript form at the high altar was the mappemonde. Two surviving examples, from Hereford Cathedral (the Hereford Mappa Mundi in Hereford Cathedral) and North Creake Abbey in Norfolk (the Aslake Map in the British Library), were actually used as altarpieces, or reredos, and served as visual encylopaedias of medieval lore concerning God's temporal plan for the world, with Jerusalem firmly located at the centre, Eden at the top, and with the marginal territories inhabited by the mythical races discussed in early Christian texts such as the Marvels of the east, in which they, and exotic local flora and fauna, are imbued with Christian moralistic symbolism.

Another case of a book serving as a virtual altar may be the Crucifixion miniature in the Sherborne Missal,[28] made at the Benedictine Abbey of St Mary's in Sherborne, Dorset, at the beginning of the fifteenth century.[29] This is the only full-page illumination in the book and its stands opposite a blank folio, allowing it to function, without distraction, as a spatial focus of public and private devotion like the

---

27 On all of which, see Brown, *Manuscripts from the Anglo-Saxon Age*.

28 British Library, Add. MS 74236, p. 380.

29 J. M. Backhouse, *The Sherborne Missal* (London, 1999); BL / M. P. Brown, *The Sherborne Missal on Turning the Pages*, CD-Rom, London, 2001; for the Sherborne Missal, the Luttrell Psalter, the Lindisfarne Gospels and other manuscripts on the 'turning the pages system', see www.bl.uk, 'treasures online'.

altarpieces of the age, which are painted in similar 'International Gothic' style. Elsewhere in this imposing volume, the illuminations of which would fill the national gallery if they were of the scale of their panel-painting counterparts, we can witness attempts by medieval artists and their patrons to site themselves within biblical space. The leading patron, Abbot Robert Bruyning, is depicted some 100 times, often in an attitude of prayer, vested as a humble Benedictine, or in the liturgical pomp of Sherborne's best copes, associating himself with adjacent depictions of Christ inviting his disciples to enter the celestial kingdom, or, along with other members of the team, joining the heavenly ranks in their joyful union with the Trinity on the page depicting the Order of the Mass for Trinity Sunday. For the feast of the Nativity,[30] the Virgin is shown having given birth, not in a Palestinian stable, but in Abbot Bruyning's own chamber, identified by the devices on the tapestry hangings, attended by a midwife who has stepped straight off the fashionable streets of fifteenth-century Sherborne. Even the margins of this grand book are turned into sacred space, when, at the central Canon of the Mass, they are occupied by a choir of native British birds (copied from a sketchbook perhaps made for Durham Cathedral and featuring coastal species such as the gannet), who sing along with the musical notation as part of a choir of Creation praising its maker.

Liminal space in the margins could also be used in Gothic manuscripts to depict the less sacred aspects of worship and society. In the Luttrell Psalter, for example,[31] made in the 1330s for Sir Geoffrey Luttrell of the manor of Irnham, Lincs. on the eve of the Black Death, the marginal counter serves as a space wherein dwells a bizarre race of grotesques – nightmarish hybrid figures parodying human folly, which represent the forces of chaos ever ready to be unleashed and to overturn the divine order, of which Sir Geoffrey saw himself the local guarantor on the manorial landscape. He also had himself depicted

---

30 Sherborne Missal, British Library, Add. MS 74236, p. 542.

31 British Library, Add. MS 42130. See the facsimile with commentary by M. P. Brown, *The Luttrell Psalter* (London, 2006). See also J. M. Backhouse, *The Luttrell Psalter* (London, 1989); M. Camille, *Image on the Edge: The Margins of Medieval Art* (London, 1992); *Mirror in Parchment: The Luttrell Psalter and the Making of Medieval England* (London, 1998).

astride his war-horse, ready for battle, but this time not on behalf of his ruler but, in his later life, as a *miles Christi* ('soldier of Christ') facing the spiritual fray. That local world is likewise portrayed within the margins, with the great family, their servants and serfs and other contemporary figures and events jostling around the margins of the sacred space of the text itself, with its more established programme of biblical iconographies contained within its 'story-telling' initials (or, as they are properly called, historiated initials). And yet the figures of tinkers and troubadours, of the disabled, the poor and the dispossessed are not banished to liminal space but serve as reminders to wealthy bibliophiles of the scriptural implications for issues of social justice and personal conscience. Not so surprising, given the role of the mendicant preachers amongst the leading illuminators and spiritual counsellors of the day. And in any event, medieval narrative images are seldom to be taken solely at face value. The medieval thought process did not stop at one literal meaning, but preferred to strip off the layers of symbolic and metaphorical meaning, like an onion, to reach the core. Thus the figures of medieval ploughmen and other agricultural workers who labour in the lower margins of the Luttrell Psalter are not only there to indicate the range of rural society, or the imminent threat of social unrest, but are ploughing the ground to receive the seed of the Word and to raise up new souls to the Lord. At all levels, such images serve to complement those from biblical narrative within the text and bring the medieval viewer into a more direct personal relationship with the Psalms, making them continually relevant to the age.[32]

This tradition of medieval people associating themselves and their situations of dilemma, pain and joy with scripture and situating themselves within the biblical landscape has a long ancestry. Bede (died 735) and the later Anglo-Saxon homilist Aelfric, writing around 1000 in the face of renewed Viking attack, acknowledged the Christian debt to the Jews for sharing their scripture, and encouraged their contemporaries similarly to share the 'Good News' (Old English 'Godspell'). They wrote of the Anglo-Saxons as the new children of

---

32   Luttrell Psalter, British Library, Add. MS 42130, f. 170r.

Israel, who shared a sense of exile and journey, having left their native Germanic homelands for their promised land. Illustrations of the Genesis narrative in the Junius Manuscript (Oxford, Bodleian Library, MS Junius 11), made in Canterbury around 1000 accordingly depict Adam and Eve and their offspring as Anglo-Saxon figures in contemporary dress.[33]

Around this time another Canterbury scribe, Eadui Basan (Eadui 'the fat'), devised his own novel approach to locating himself in relation to sacred space. In the Arundel Psalter,[34] which he is thought to have written and illuminated in the early eleventh century, he depicts himself in obeisance at the feet of St Benedict, founder of his monastic order. The enthroned figure of Benedict is fully painted and gilded, whereas the wraithlike figures of the monks of Christ Church Canterbury, to whom he hands a copy of his monastic rule, are in ethereal tinted drawing, the difference in technique probably being intended to draw a distinction between fully-painted sacred space and the temporal space in which the brethren, living or dead, dwell. It is typical of Eadui – who appears to have been a particularly colourful character spending much time away from the cloister writing documents and de luxe books for King Cnut and his circle – that even though his bottom spans the two zones, it is fully painted and sacred by association.[35]

Moving, finally, from considerations of sacred and temporal space to that of space – 'the final frontier' – it is instructive to consider the role of '*influxus stellarum*', the influence of the stars, which to the medieval mind could mean the agency of sacred space and the means by which divine will was enacted, the superglue holding together Creation, part of a medieval 'theory of everything', but asking the how as well as the why.[36] Although limited in its extent, this mode of thought is somewhat reminiscent of the way in which the language of

33   B. J. Muir, *Bodleian, MS Junius 11*, CD-Rom, Bodleian Digital Texts 1 (Oxford, 2004).

34   British Library, Arundel MS 155, f. 133r.

35   Brown, *Manuscripts from the Anglo-Saxon Age*.

36   For a fuller discussion of the following, see M. P. Brown, 'An Early Outbreak of 'Influenza'? Aspects of Influence, Medieval and Modern', in A. Bovey, ed., *Under the Influence* (Turnhout, 2006).

modern quantum physics is increasingly growing to resemble that of theology. In medieval depictions of the stars and their constellations, accompanying texts such as the *Aratea*, Cicero's Latin translation of the Greek *Phaenomena* of Aratus (as in B.L., Harl. MS 2506, illustrated by an Anglo-Saxon artist collaborating with the French scriptorium of Fleury, *c*.1000),[37] classical mythology concerning their interpretation was preserved as part of a Christian conceptualization of their role in exerting the divine will through their influence, or 'pull'.

The origins of this concept of an external agency directing human action and will is probably as old as humankind and is found in the Bible in Job 33.31, which in the Geneva version of 1560 is translated as 'Canst thou restraine the sweete influences of the Pleiades?' This motif is echoed by Milton in 1667 in his *Paradise Lost*, vii.375, when he writes 'The Pleiades before him danc'd, Shedding sweet influence'. The transmission of this literary mode of visualization to the modern world was, of course, assured by Shakespeare's 'star-crossed lovers'. A complex inter-relationship between astronomy and astrology pervaded medieval life and art. A visual affirmation of this link is found prefacing many a devotional and scientific book in the form of the perpetual link between time, the land, the lives of those who inhabit and labour upon it and the influences of the stars, symbolized by the Kalendar, with its accompanying zodiac symbols and labours of the months.

As ideas changed in the realms both of physics and of metaphysics, so the principle of *influxus physicus*, physical influence, developed, denoting the exertion of action of which the operation is unseen, or perceptible only in its effects, by one person or thing upon another: Shakespeare's 'gibing spirit, Whose influence is begot of that loose grace, Which shallow laughing hearers give to fooles' (*Loves Labours Lost*, V.ii.866–8). In 1603 Francis Bacon summarized its rationalization within the modern world as: 'The wisdom of conversation . . . hath . . . an influence also into business and government' (*The Advancement of Learning*, II.xxiii parag. 3).[38]

---

37   See Brown, *Manuscripts from the Anglo-Saxon Age*.
38   Francis Bacon, *The Advancement of Learning*, M. Kiernan, ed. (Oxford, 2000).

Overarching all of this during the Middle Ages was the concept, transcending that of space and its constraints, of the inflowing or infusion into a person or thing of divine, spiritual, moral or immaterial power or principle – *influentia divina*, a concept encountered in the Bible, Wisdom 7.25, 'She is the breath of the power of God, and a pure influence flowing from the glory of the Almighty'. This belief is encountered increasingly from the thirteenth century and was expounded by Aquinas, around 1260, as '*influentia causae*', a scholastic enshrinement of the principle of cause and effect, introduced to northern Europe by its implicit pervasion of the writings of Bede. This was essentially a Christianization of the classical idea of a 'prime mover', described by Thomas Aylesbury in his *Sermons* of 1623, as 'The unknowne God, whose influence to all his Creatures was made known by the Poet'.[39] The role of literature and art in conveying the mystery of the invisible force that binds all things together across time and space has always been a fundamental one. They found one of their most powerful and graphic manifestations in the medieval illuminated book.

---

39 Thomas Aylesbury, *Paganisme and Papisme: Parallel'd and Set Forth in a Sermon at the Temple Church* (London, 1624).

Chapter 4

The World Shall Come to Walsingham

Timothy Radcliffe

I have never walked on pilgrimage to Walsingham, but every year some Dominican brethren set off on 'Student Cross', in which groups of twenty or thirty students start from various places and converge on Walsingham, carrying large crosses, for the celebration of Easter. When I was a young friar I was often invited to go, but was always told by my community that I was needed at Blackfriars that year; I would be free the following year, they said, but I never was. So those who can, walk, and those who can't, talk.

My purpose in this essay is to talk about language as a sacred place. It is a wonderful subject, but, since I have no special expertise at all in the area, I may not be the best equipped discussant. However, the great advantage of the celibate life is that one can read novels in bed at night as long as one likes: that is my only qualification.

I start with a poem by Robert Lowell, 'Our Lady of Walsingham':

> There once the penitents took off their shoes
> And then walked barefoot the remaining mile;
> And the small trees, a stream and hedgerows file
> Slowly along the munching English lane,
> Like cows to the old shrine, until you lose
> Track of your dragging pain.
> The stream flows down under the druid tree,
> Shiloah's whirlpools gurgle and make glad
> The castle of God. Sailor, you were glad
> And whistled Sion by that stream. But see:

Our Lady, too small for her canopy,
Sits near the altar. There's no comeliness
at all or charm in that expressionless
Face with its heavy eyelids. As before,
This face, for centuries a memory,
Non est species, neque decor,
Expressionless, expresses God: it goes
Past castled Sion. She knows what God knows,
Not Calvary's Cross nor crib at Bethlehem
Now, and the world shall come to Walsingham.[1]

This is a poem about pilgrimage. It evokes the penitents who walked to the shrine barefoot through the 'munching English lane'. But the poem is *itself* a pilgrimage. It evokes Jerusalem, the original sacred space, as Margaret Barker's essay[2] shows. It mentions Calvary's Cross and the crib at Bethlehem. But it propels us forward to what God knows *now*, '. . . and the world shall come to Walsingham'. It celebrates a place of pilgrimage but evokes that more fundamental journey, which is that of humanity to the Kingdom.

One way of understanding that journey is our slow entry into conversation with God. We need time to learn to be at home in the limitlessness of God's word. None of us who are native to this country can remember the years it took for us to learn to speak English. Slowly we found ourselves at home in our tongue. We learn to be at ease within the conversations of our families and their friends. This is the greatest gift we receive, a language in which we can speak and hear love. Similarly, human history is the journey home, nesting ourselves within the conversation which is the Trinity, whose Word is made flesh in Jesus.

In 1996, Yiyun Li left China. When she arrived in the United States she could not speak a word of English, but she learned fast. In a short story called, 'A thousand years of good prayers' a Chinese daughter

---

1   Robert Lowell, 'Our Lady of Walsingham', in *Collected Poems 1917–77* (London, 2003), pp. 17–18.
2   See below, pp. 81–99.

tries to explain to her father why she can only talk about her divorce in English. She says, 'Baba, if you grew up in a language that you never used to express your feelings, it would be easier to take up another language and talk more in the new language. It makes you a new person.'[3] Our pilgrimage to the Kingdom is learning a language in which we can be new people, a language in which we can flourish and be free.

Every Christmas we sing the genealogy of Christ. It goes on and on. I find myself counting on my fingers, to see how many more begettings there must be before Jesus arrives. Will it never be over? But it took all that time for there to be a language in which the Word could be made flesh. It took centuries of people struggling to put into word praise and dejection, victories and defeats, liberation and exile, before the language was ready to receive the Word made flesh. It took all those prophets and scribes, soldiers and farmers, husbands and wives before the language was ready to be fertilized by the Spirit. There were generations of unknown people, borrowing words from foreigners, from Egyptians and Canaanites, Babylonians and Persians, Greeks and Romans, reshaping them for Israel's faith. Jesus could no more have been born earlier than one could expect a baby Shakespeare to write *Hamlet*. The gestation of the Word took centuries. And the Incarnation is not the end of the story. We are still learning how to be at home in God's Word. It is still stretching open our language, so that it may be capacious enough for God. God became flesh in our words, and we are still learning to be at home in his Word.

In this essay I will very briefly evoke something of the journey that was made within the covers of the Bible, leading up to Jesus. I will be very brief, first of all because I am not a scriptural scholar and do not want to put my foot in it; and, secondly, because, like Mary at Walsingham, I wish to concentrate on the linguistic pilgrimage that we are still engaged in, trying to glimpse what God knows *now*, 'and the world shall come to Walsingham'.

---

3   Yiyun Li, *A Thousand Years of Good Prayers: Stories by Yiyun Li* (London, 2005) p. 199.

Most people, when they begin to read the Bible, expect to learn facts. Fundamentalist Christians read Genesis to learn facts about the creation of the world. And even if one grows beyond a literal interpretation of the Bible, one may still hope for facts about God. But the Bible is not primarily *about* God. Rather it is entering into conversation with God. What matters is not so much the accuracy of the text as the fidelity of the speaker, who transforms us by engaging us in conversation. Gabriel Josipovici says, 'We have to trust the book itself and see where it will take us . . . The Bible guides us if we will only let it, towards the answers it contains but can only show, not tell'.[4] One surrenders to the narrative, and it carries us onwards, towards a revelation that is always somehow in the future, yet to be fully given.

The Good News Bible promised a translation that was 'clear, simple, and unambiguous'.[5] That was a misguided promise, because the beauty and power of the Bible is precisely that it is not clear, simple and unambiguous. Its language is suggestive, allusive, puzzling – resembling a conversation with someone who is always leading one on to a disclosure that promises to make sense of everything.

The words of the biblical authors are not simply written down and frozen. They evolve and develop, like trees headed towards the light. Valéry said that a poem is never completed, just abandoned.[6] The prophecy of Isaiah grew over generations, constantly being adapted, extended. It is rather like Mrs Beeton. Long after the original sturdy Victorian matron died, her corpus continues to flourish, with new books appearing all the time. When I read of 'Mrs Beeton's microwave cooking', I thought of Trito-Isaiah! So the words of the Bible are themselves on a pilgrimage, headed towards the Word made flesh. This means that they are moving downwards and outwards.

The Bible brings God down to earth, literally. Think of Mount Zion. Other religions had their sacred mythological mountains, represented by the ziggurats. Israel had little Zion, 'the hill which he

---

4   G. Josipovici, *The Book of God: A Response to the Bible* (New Haven, 1988), pp. 27–8.

5   S. Pritchard, *Words and The Word* (Cambridge, 1986), p. 4.

6   Quoted by Josipovici, *op. cit.*, p. 10.

loves' (Psalm 78.68). It was an insignificant pimple of a hillock, but it is a real one. It is not an imitation of a mountain in the heavens. It is where God has chosen to dwell with his people.

And God does not just come down to earth. God becomes entangled with Israel. Think for a moment of the Song of Deborah in Judges 5. When I was a student, this was considered to be one of the oldest passages in the Bible. It describes God as a warrior, coming to defeat the enemies of Israel:

> Lord, when thou didst go forth from Se'ir,
> when thou didst march from the region of Edom,
> the earth trembled, and the heavens dropped water.
> The mountains quaked before the Lord,
> Yon Sinai before the Lord, the God of Israel.[7]

He is a storm God, who pours down rain to fertilize the earth. He is a warrior God, zapping the enemy with his lightning. This is just the sort of God that you could find in the mythologies of the neighbouring peoples, such as the Canaanites. These religions of fertility and war told the stories of the gods, how they fought and made love, sulked and feasted. Israel borrowed the language, but Israel came slowly to understand that their God was not just the top God, but the only God. And that meant that there could not be any stories of the gods. The God of Israel did not have any other gods to fight against or make love to. The only story that could be told about our God was the story of his involvement with his chosen people.

The song of Deborah ends with the words: 'So perish all thine enemies, O Lord, But thy friends be like the sun as he rises in his might' (5.31). Some scholars suggest that 'lovers' might be a better translation. God's only lovers are the Israelites; he has no goddess to marry. The only love story is not a mythology, but the story of Israel. One might therefore say that the language of the Bible is, from a very early date, like a heat-seeking missile, searching for our flesh, headed towards incarnation.

---

7 Judges 5.4–5.

So the dynamism of the text is towards intimacy, God drawing close to us. In the book of Deuteronomy we read, 'For what great nation is there that has a god so near to it as the Lord our God is to us, whenever we call upon him' (4.7). Moses says to the Israelites, 'The word is very near you; it is in your mouth and in your heart, so that you can do it' (30.14). When the Word becomes flesh in Jesus, it is astonishing, utterly unexpected, previously unimaginable. And yet, with hindsight, we can see that it was always coming this way. The words have been growing towards this moment, in which the Word of God becomes a human being, one of us. We see the one who talks to us face to face.

But the movement of the text is not just earthwards, towards incarnation; it is also outwards, towards universality. As we have seen already, there could only be one God and one story for Israel; for the same reason, if there is just the one God of the universe, then this story was not just about Israel, but about all the world, which shall one day come to Walsingham. Slowly the Bible edges its way towards the awareness that there is only one story for all of creation. The covenant with Abraham was to be the blessing of all nations. Isaiah can even make the incredible claim that Egypt and Assyria are beloved of God, his people too. 'In that day Israel will be the third with Egypt and Assyria, a blessing in the midst of the earth, whom of the Lord of hosts has blessed saying. "Blessed be Egypt my people, and Assyria the work of my hands, and Israel, my heritage"' (19.24).

So my thesis, vastly oversimplified, is that the slow dawning of monotheism generates this double movement. There are no stories of the gods. There is just the story of God's entanglement with this particular people, his chosen nation, Israel. And the story of Israel is not just of a particular people, but of God's relationship with humanity. And this double movement towards the particular and the universal finds its astonishing culmination in that particular human being whom the Father declares his beloved and in whom he delights. You cannot get more particular than that! But this particular being is the one in whom, according to St Paul, 'there is neither Jew nor Greek, there is neither slave nor free, there is neither male nor female' (Galatians 3.28). Christ is the one in whom there is a place for everyone. He is both unique and universal.

But the journey does not end there. The Word has been made flesh and dwelt among us, but all the rest of history will be catching up with this event. When we meditate on the Word of God, we are like the python in *Le Petit Prince* which has swallowed an elephant, which is stretching it almost to bursting. The Bible does offer us a religious language in which to speak of God. It offers God's words about God. But it does more than that. It invites us to converse with God, to enter into a conversation which stretches open our ways of talking. We are forever searching for words that will let us delight in the particular and reach out to the universal. The movement that we saw beginning in the Old Testament and finding its culmination in the New carries on. We go on searching for words that are precise enough for the particularity of Jesus and spacious enough for his universality.

How does this happen? When Jesus emerges from the waters of baptism, according to Mark's gospel he hears the voice from heaven which says, 'Thou art my beloved Son; with whom I am well pleased' (1.11). It all begins with the delight of the Father in the Son. The ministry of Jesus begins with his delight in us, in tax collectors and prostitutes, in Roman centurions and even, if they will but let him, in Pharisees. We have to learn the language of delight, taking pleasure not just in Jesus but in each other.

One of the ways in which we do so is through reading literature. A student once asked Dorothy Day, when she was very old and famous, 'What is the meaning of your life? How would you like to be remembered?' She replied that she would like to be thought of as having treated the stranger as Christ, and as having lived a life worthy of the great novels she had read. 'I'd like people to say that "she really did love those books!" You know, I am always telling people to read Dickens or Tolstoi, or read Orwell or Silone . . . That's the meaning of my life – to live up to the moral vision of the Church, and of some of my favourite writers . . . to take those artists and novelists to heart, and to live up to their wisdom.'[8]

Literature opens our eyes to God's pleasure in his creatures.

---

8   Quoted in P. Elie, *The Life You Save May Be Your Own: An American Pilgrimage* (New York, 2003), p. 452.

Nicholas Boyle argues that not only is the Bible literature, but that literature is scripture. He writes: 'A book becomes literature by using language for the purposeless purpose of enjoyment. But language is the medium of the Law, of the Word which tells us that everything matters, even the sparrows on the rooftops. By showing life as mattering, and thus sharing in the work of the Spirit, literature enables us to take pleasure in a truth about human existence: the truth that its constitution is inescapably moral'.[9]

G. K. Chesterton, like Dorothy Day, enjoyed Charles Dickens, and Dickens enjoyed everyone, the good, the bad and the ugly, especially the bad and the ugly. Chesterton wrote: 'The art of Dickens was the most exquisite of arts: it was the art of enjoying everybody . . . I do not for a moment maintain that he enjoyed everybody in his daily life. But he enjoyed everybody in his books; and everybody has enjoyed everybody in those books even till today'.[10]

If we are taught to delight in people, then we learn to see them as God sees them, even if the novelist or poet is not a believer. For George Mackay Brown, however, his poetry was profoundly part of his relationship with God. Even though he lived alone, 'every one was the writer's concern. The whole of humanity is his family and he must participate in their joys and ennuis and sufferings, otherwise what he does would be as meaningless as an endless game of patience'.[11] If we share God's pleasure in people, then they became part of our relationship with God, part of our prayer. Boyle again: 'By showing the world as mattering to somebody, they show it as a matter for prayer, the general prayer "for all sorts and conditions of men" which takes those who utter it across the frontier between the secular and the sacred and is the first word of reconciliation between God and the world'.[12]

---

9 N. Boyle, *Sacred and Secular Scriptures: A Catholic Approach to Literature* (London, 2004), p. 131.

10 G. K. Chesterton, *The Victorian Age in Literature* (London, 1912), p. 119; cf. Boyle, op. cit., p. 131.

11 Quoted by Maggie Ferguson in 'Gathering Jewels', *The Tablet*, 15 April 2006, p. 19.

12 Boyle, op. cit., p. 182.

Marilynne Robinson achieves this wonderfully in her latest novel, *Gilead*. An old Protestant Pastor in the Deep South of the United States is approaching death. He sends for his son, to share with him his store of wisdom before it is too late. Much of it is about taking pleasure in the existence of things. I must struggle to resist quoting vast chunks of this marvellous book. He says:

'I have been thinking about existence lately. In fact I have been so full of admiration for existence that I have hardly been able to enjoy it properly.' He talks of some oak trees that he has seen. 'It was a very clear night, or morning, very still, and then there was such energy in the things transpiring among those trees, like travail. I stood there a little out of range, and I thought, it is all still new to me. I have lived my life on the prairie and a line of oak trees can still astonish me. I feel sometimes as if I were a child who opens its eyes on the world once and sees amazing things it will never know any names for and then has to close its eyes again.'[13]

Above all it is his son in whom, like God, he delights:

'There's a shimmer on a child's hair, in the sunlight. There are rainbow colours in it, tiny, soft beams of just the same colours you can see in the dew sometimes. They're in the petal of flowers, and they're on a child's skin. Your hair is straight and dark, and your skin is very fair. I suppose you're not much prettier than most children. You're just a nice-looking boy, a bit slight, well scrubbed and well mannered. All that is fine, but it's your existence I love you for, mainly.'[14]

So literature carries on, as it were, the momentum of God's word, homing in on the particular, taking pleasure in what Louis MacNeice calls 'the drunkenness of things being various'.[15] It helps us to share

---

13   Marilynne Robinson, *Gilead* (New York, 2004), pp. 56f.
14   Ibid., p. 136.
15   Louis MacNeice, 'Snow', line 8, in *The Collected Poems of Louis MacNeice* (London, 1966), p. 30.

in God's pure pleasure in the individuality of his creatures. But literature may also offer us a taste of the universality of Christ. It opens our hearts and minds to the utter diversity of ways of being human. One of the great pleasures of my nine years of visiting the Order in more than a hundred countries was tasting the utter variety of the world's literatures. I discovered the sheer pleasure of reading the crazy, fantastic literatures of Latin America, of Jorge Luis Borges, Gabriel Garcia Marquez, Isabelle Allende, Mario Vargas Llosa. This opens us up just a little more to the spaciousness of the Kingdom, the vastness of God. So it is not just that Christianity can express itself within these literatures. They deepen our sense of what it might mean to be part of Christ, in whom there is neither Jew nor Gentile, male nor female, slave nor free.

Just think of the Black Christian culture of the American South. That experience of enslavement and liberation extends our understanding of what it means to die and rise in Christ. The Black theologian J. Kameron Carter says that black existence is: '"a" word of God, just to the extent that it is an articulation of "the" Word of God. It is a "word" within the Word.'[16] Black life extends our vocabulary. It gives us a language that is that tiny bit more capacious. It is another step towards the Word becoming all flesh. It adds another colour to our palate. Carter writes, 'Black life is an inflection and so an articulation of the Eternal Word'.[17] Its pain and joy is his.

Often novelists are doing more than just sharing with us a delight that they have attained. The writing is part of the labour of coming to love. They may search for words not to describe the love that they have but so as to discover it. This is a discipline of attentiveness, learning to see the goodness that had been hidden. We can write our way into compassion. John Burnside is a Scottish poet, whose life was overshadowed by his father, whom he hated so much that he even planned to kill him. When John himself had a son, he knew that the time had come to reconcile himself with his own father. And this

---

16   J. Kameron Carter, quoted in Rupert Shortt (ed.) *God's Advocates: Christian Thinkers in Conversation* (London, 2005), pp. 239–40.

17   Shortt, *op. cit.* p. 241.

must happen through his writing. The book *A Lie about My Father* moves towards this conclusion, this new compassion, given one Halloween:

> In the memory that comes this Halloween, my father is not the brutal, unhappy drunk I knew best, the man who passed his days in a fog of bewilderment, wondering who was to blame for his inconsequentiality, but someone I must have caught a glimpse of, back in Cowdenbeath, even if I don't remember exactly when it was, or why he was there, standing outside our house one night, alone in the dark, rain dripping from the trees around him. In this memory he has his back to me, but I sense a stillness, a deep quiet that is not necessarily that of a man at rest, as he stands at the edge of Mr Kirk's woods, lighting a cigarette, nameless and, for a moment, free to be whoever he wishes. There must be some ordinary reason why he is out there in the wet, a few feet from his front door, but that isn't what matters now. What matters is that I can see him again, in his white shirt, and I know he is different from the man I learned to fear, the man I wanted to kill. I know his being there is an unusual event, one I may even have misunderstood – in this memory I am, perhaps, four or five – but it is important that I remember him exactly like this, because this is the father I could bring myself to forgive.[18]

This struggle to find words for love and forgiveness is part of our reaching forward to the Kingdom, when the whole of creation will be gathered in. This is the plenitude for which we have no adequate words; it is what Mary contemplates in Lowell's poem, what God knows now, and the world shall come to Walsingham. It is best evoked poetically, as Isaiah does with images of when:

> . . . the wolf shall dwell with the lamb, and the leopard shall lie
> down with the kid,
> And the calf and the lion and the fatling together

---

18   John Burnside, *A Lie about My Father* (London, 2006), p. 323.

And a little child shall lead them . . .
They shall not hurt or destroy in all my holy mountain;
For the earth shall be full of the knowledge of the Lord as the
   waters cover the sea. (11.6–9)

In the story 'Revelation' by Flannery O'Connor, we meet Mrs
Turpin, a fat lady of the Deep South, deeply fascinated by gradations
of status, who gives thanks to Jesus that she is neither black nor white
trash. In fact she loves to wonder which would be worse. And then a
crisis is provoked when an ugly girl in the doctor's waiting room
hurls a book at her and calls her an old wart hog from hell. It is a
moment of truth that leads to revelation, as she is cleaning down the
real live hogs on her small farm. She sees a purple streak in the sky:

A visionary light settled in her eyes. She saw the streak as a vast
swinging bridge extending upwards from the earth through a field
of living fire. Upon it a vast horde of souls were rumbling towards
heaven. There were companies of white-trash, clean for the first
time in their lives, and bands of black niggers in white robes, and
battalions of freaks and lunatics shouting and clapping and
leaping like frogs. And bringing up the end of the procession was
a tribe of people whom she recognised at once as those who, like
herself and Claud, had always had a little of everything and the
God-given wit to use it right. She leaned forward to observe them
closer. They were marching behind the others with great dignity,
accountable as they had always been for good order, common
sense and respectable behaviour. They alone were on key. Yet she
could see by their shocked and altered faces that even their virtues
were being burnt away. She lowered her hands and gripped the rail
of the hog pen, her eyes small but fixed unblinkingly on what lay
ahead.[19]

---

19   Flannery O'Connor, 'Revelation' in *The Complete Stories of Flannery O'Connor* (New
York, 1971), p. 508.

So we leave her there, with the hogs, with her little piggy eyes fixed on what lay ahead. She is on her pilgrimage. She is herself Flannery O'Connor, in whose letters there are signs of old Southern white bigotry, but whose writing pushes ahead of herself, towards a new world, which she does not yet inhabit herself but can suggest in her stories.[20] Her writing is part of her pilgrimage and of her own transformation. She is propelled forward, towards becoming the sort of person who could write such a story.

But there is more. Jesus did not just express God's delight in his children. He embraced those who were shut out, the ritually impure – the lepers, the sinners, the unholy. If the Temple was the sacred space of Israel, then our sacred space, our new Temple, Jesus, is the one who embraces the unholy. Our sacrifice is performed on the hill outside the city, on that cursed instrument of torture that is the cross. As St Paul wrote, he became a curse for us (Galatians 3.13). So this is an utterly new understanding of holiness: holiness not as separation from what is unclean, but as proximity.

So the embrace of what is secular and pagan is part of the Christian pilgrimage to the Kingdom. The early Christians go to Rome – seeing it as Babylon, the city of the enemy Empire – and it becomes our eternal City, a holy city. The Holy Father takes the name of the pagan priest, Pontifex Maximus. Boyle writes: 'The presence of what is alien, pagan, unholy, unclean at the heart of the church is essential to its nature. When the Church finds what is unholy, then it must say "For this too Christ died" ... In such moments the Church too must die, must swallow its pride, give up the boundary which it thought defined its existence, and discover a new and larger vocation. And that new vocation will itself be defined by a new boundary which in time the Church will also have to transcend'.

When St Augustine of Canterbury came to convert the English, Gregory the Great wrote:

---

20   cf. Elie, op.cit., p. 327.

Tell Augustine that he should by no means destroy the temples of the gods but rather the idols within those temples. Let him, after he has purified them with holy water, place altars and relics of the saints in them. For, if those temples are well built, they should be converted from the worship of demons to the service of the true God. Thus, seeing that their places of worship are not destroyed, the people will banish error from their hearts and come to places familiar and dear to them in acknowledgement and worship of the true God.[21]

And when the missionaries went to the Americas they found the worship of the seed god, whose power was shown in the fertility of maize, such as Xilonen, the female corn god, known as the Hairy one.[22] So they made crosses of the sacred corn pith, so that the old religion of fertility was caught up in the new faith in death and resurrection. What, we must ask, is secular or pagan in our society that we may embrace? Who are the gods whose emblems we can claim in the name of one God? Who are the Egyptians whom we may spoil? The Catholic bishops of England and Wales, for example, are resisting the temptation to demonize *The Da Vinci Code*; they have been thinking instead how to use the publicity for evangelization. As their spokesman said, 'Let's turn lemon into lemonade'.

According to John (15.7), Jesus said to the disciples on the night before he died: 'If you abide in me, and my words abide in you, ask whatever you will, and it shall be done for you'. This is a mutual abiding. We make our home in Jesus and we let his words be at home in us. The Bible does not principally offer us information, facts about God or Jesus. It does more than just give us a language in which to believe and worship. It offers a conversation that is not over, as we reach towards God's delight in the particularity of all that exists, and the universality of the Kingdom. We never stop sharing in God's embrace of everything that stands outside the camp. The Word of

---

21   Gregory I, *Letter to Abbot Mellitus* = *Epistola* 76, *Patrologia Latina* (Migne ed.) 77: 1215–1216.

22   A. B. Gauvin, *Art of Colonial Latin America* (London, 2005), p. 101.

God challenges all the smallness and the pettiness in how we speak, all the domination and exclusion. It purifies our language of contempt and denigration.

The Word was made flesh two thousand years ago, but we are still trying to catch up with the vision of Mary:

> She knows what God knows,
> Not Calvary's Cross nor crib at Bethlehem
> Now, and the world shall come to Walsingham.

My ending is a poem by an Irish Dominican, Paul Murray, that articulates a partial sense of what happens when one starts talking to God, or at least to God's angels!

> The text opens like a river
> in full spate. Or, it's like a window
> opening with a sudden gust of wind.
> And it's as if an archangel
> had entered the room. And everybody
> has to stop what they're doing.
> And the air is a river of divine words.
> And all of a sudden you see
> – and with a start –
> that an archangel *has* entered,
> and your heart is in your mouth.
> And you feel you are drowning
> in a river of divine words, and hear
> yourself saying, over and over,
> 'How can this be?'[23]

---

23   P. Murray, published here for the first time, by permission of the author.

Chapter 5

The House Within a House

Margaret Barker

The first time I visited the shrine at Walsingham, it was curiously familiar. In this chapter, I will try to show you why.

A temple stood in Jerusalem for over 1,000 years, as the centre of the world and as the world view of those who wrote most of the Bible. There were in fact several temples: one built by Solomon, and destroyed by the Babylonians at the beginning of the sixth century BC, another built by the exiles who returned from Babylon, and there was a massive refurbishment in the time of Herod the Great which was almost a third temple. This third temple is the one mentioned in John's gospel: 'It has taken forty-six years to build this temple and will you raise it up again in three days?' (John 2.20).

Each temple caused controversy: the writer of the Books of Kings, influenced by the ideals of Deuteronomy, thought the temple an extravagant mistake, plunging the kingdom into debt and the people into forced labour (1 Kings 5.13–18 and 9.10–14, showing how Solomon paid the debt), which caused such resentment that ten tribes revolted from Solomon's heir and the kingdom was split (1 Kings 11.26–40). The same writer thought that the monarchy itself was an institution alien to their tradition (1 Samuel 8.4–22) and chose his material to show how wicked most of the kings had been. The second temple was equally controversial, but most of the objections are recorded in books that did not become part of the Bible. The people who built the second temple had made massive changes in the religious traditions of their people, and conservative voices

(Isaiah 57.7–8) called that temple a harlot who had taken money for rebuilding from the Persian kings but was not prepared to accept the ancient worshippers of the LORD. Hostility to Herod's temple can be seen, for example, in the story of Jesus cleansing it, or in the vision of the burning harlot in the Book of Revelation (Revelation 19.1–3).

Such a chequered history means that the written sources have to be handled with care, especially by Christian scholars, since the roots of Christianity lie in what we might call the excluded tradition, and yet historically Christian scholars have been, and in some cases still are, limited to using materials in a canon both composed and compiled by another tradition. Many of the canonical records of the first temple were compiled by people hostile to the monarchy, which is the root of all notions of the Messiah, and hostile to the temple, which is the ultimate setting for Christian liturgy. When the story of Moses and the desert tabernacle was compiled, it was coloured by memories of the temple, and so in many cases tabernacle tradition reflects that of the temple. The objections to the second temple and its innovations are largely preserved in the non-canonical texts, which until recently were either unknown or excluded from the discussion.

Despite the controversies, both ancient and modern, and the necessary complexity of scholarly reconstructions, it is clear that the temple stood at the centre of the worldview that became the Christian worldview. When Jesus said: 'Father, glorify thou me in thy own presence with the glory which I had with thee before the world was made' he was speaking within the temple worldview. When Jesus answered his critics, after healing the man at Bethsaida on the Sabbath: 'My Father is working still and I am working' (John 5.17) he was speaking within the temple time-frame. The concept of the Kingdom of God, central to all Jesus's teaching, is rooted in temple tradition. In the Book of Revelation, the woman clothed with the sun who gave birth to the Messiah appeared in the temple, in the holy of holies (Revelation 11.19–12.6).

Sacred Space and the Controversy Over the Temple

There had been a cultural revolution in Jerusalem and Judah at the end of the seventh century BC, in the reign of King Josiah. The account of this in 2 Kings 22–23 invites us to believe that the purges were inspired by the rediscovery of Deuteronomy, and the changes are presented as a great purification and reform to conform to the requirements of Deuteronomy. The story of the Davidic kings in 1 and 2 Kings is a pessimistic and highly critical overview of the national history. The spiritual heirs of the Deuteronomists were deeply hostile both to the monarchy and to the temple. Traditional material was reworked in a new setting, and the new ideas are unmistakable: the LORD no longer lived in the holy of holies.

When Solomon consecrated the temple, the Deuteronomists included what looks like an ancient prayer of dedication. Solomon said: 'I have built thee an exalted house, a place for thee to dwell in for ever' (1 Kings 8.13), which echoes the LORD's command to Moses: 'Let them make me a holy place that I may dwell in their midst' (Exodus 25.8). The later editor in effect contradicted the first statement, and Solomon's dedication prayer continued: 'But will God indeed dwell on earth? Behold heaven and the highest heaven cannot contain thee; how much less this house which I have built!' (1 Kings 8.27). The holy of holies was no longer the place of the presence of God, and so the later description of the temple also omitted certain features that implied residence: the holy of holies, we are told, housed the ark of the covenant and two giant cherubim (1 Kings 6.19, 23–7). It does not say that these cherubim formed the divine throne, nor that the divine presence was screened by the great curtain, the veil of the temple. The description in Chronicles, written by someone who loved the temple, says that the cherubim formed a golden chariot (1 Chronicles 28.18) and that they were screened by a veil of blue, purple and crimson fabric, woven with fine linen (2 Chronicles 3.14).

The Deuteronomists reworked several other older traditions about the holy of holies and the visions of the throne. The ancient material in Exodus 24, for example, says that Moses and the elders saw the God of Israel on Sinai, above a pavement of sapphire. Deuteronomy contradicted this: 'The LORD spoke to you out of the midst of the fire; you heard the sound of words, but saw no form. There was only a voice' (Deuteronomy 4.12). Since seeing the LORD was the focus of temple pilgrimage, this was a major innovation.

After Moses received the Ten Commandments, according to the older tradition, he was given detailed instructions about building a place of worship: 'According to all that I show you, the pattern of all the tabernacle and the pattern of all the vessels, thus shall you make them' (Exodus 25.9, translating literally). Deuteronomy contradicted this too: after Moses had received the Commandments, 'The LORD added no more' (Deuteronomy 5.22). In other words, the command to build a holy place to a particular pattern so that the LORD could dwell in the midst was simply omitted, making it quite consistent with the revised version of Solomon's prayer, which implies that the LORD did not dwell in the temple. The Deuteronomists said that the temple would be the place where the LORD put his Name and made its habitation (Deuteronomy 12.5, translating literally). Nobody knows exactly what they meant by this, but it was characteristic of their temple theology. In the earlier theology, the Name had been present in a person, the king, and not in a place. 'Blessed is he who comes with the Name of the LORD'.

Moses received a vision from the LORD about the plan of the tabernacle, and the temple version of this tradition – that King David had received the plan of the temple – appears in Chronicles. David entrusted to Solomon everything he had received from the hand of the LORD concerning the plans for the temple courts, the chambers, the treasuries, the gifts, the priestly orders and the exact weight of gold and silver for the furnishing (1 Chronicles 28.11–19). The Deuteronomists' account of the temple building does not mention it.

The Deuteronomists, in effect, secularized the holy place and the king and removed all trace of the king's mother. For them the temple was not built according to the divine plan, and was not the meeting place of heaven and earth, and was not literally the location of the throne of the LORD (Psalm 11). They discouraged interest in the affairs of the sanctuary: 'The secret things belong to the LORD our God; but the things that are revealed belong to us and to our children for ever, that we may do all the word of this law' (Deuteronomy 29.29). They forbad any veneration of the host of heaven, the angels, and even dropped the ancient title 'the LORD of Hosts', as can be seen by comparing the two accounts of Hezekiah's prayer in the temple when the Assyrians were threatening Jerusalem. Isaiah, who had himself received a temple vision of the LORD enthroned as King amidst the heavenly beings (Isaiah 6.5), recorded the prayer thus: 'O LORD of hosts, God of Israel, who art enthroned above the cherubim . . .' (Isaiah 37.16). The Deuteronomists, however, describing the same event, had Hezekiah begin his prayer: 'O LORD the God of Israel, who art enthroned above the cherubim . . .' (2 Kings 19.15). The title LORD of Hosts does not appear in the books of Moses. For the Deuteronomists, the king had simply to uphold the law of Deuteronomy, and not to be like Solomon, marrying many wives, accumulating wealth and trading in horses (Deuteronomy 17.14–20).

Despite the rewritten texts, it is possible to recover something of the original temple and its meaning, but the evidence is fragmented and the process speculative. Nevertheless, a pattern does emerge. First, the shape of the temple, which was a small structure, 20 cubits (10 metres) wide and 60 long, divided by a curtain so that the inner holy place was a cube of twenty cubits. All the temples seem to have retained this basic scheme.

The temple represented the creation, and so the compiler of Genesis would have had something in his mind very different from the literalist reading of modern creationists. Genesis 1 describes Moses' vision of the creation, which was the plan for the tabernacle. Memories of this, with slight variations, are widespread, but the basic position is that when Moses was on Sinai for six days (Exodus 24.16), he saw the process of the creation. The six days of Genesis 1 were the six days of his vision. He was then told to build the tabernacle to replicate all he had seen on the mountain – that is, the creation. This is attested in Jewish and Christian sources.[1]

---

1 Thus Philo, *Questions on Exodus*, 2.85. A summary of other Jewish evidence in L. Ginzberg, *Legends of the Jews*, (Philadelphia, 1909) vol. 1, pp. 3–46. Christian evidence e.g. Clementine Recognitions 1.27; Cosmas Indicopleustes, *A Christian Topography*, 2.35.

Traces of the ancient scheme can still be seen in Exodus 40.16–34, where Moses finally assembles all the prepared components of the tabernacle. The end of this text sequence is fragmented, the Hebrew and Greek texts differing at certain points, but the original pattern is unmistakable: the days of tabernacle building corresponded to the days of creation. Each section in Exodus 40 is marked by 'As the LORD commanded Moses', and we see that on the second day, for example, the veil was erected to screen the ark and the mercy seat, corresponding to the firmament of heaven in Genesis separating the upper creation from the lower. There is a similar correspondence for the third day and the fourth. The fifth day is where there are text problems, and the sixth day is the creation of Adam and the purification of the high priest. The temple was Eden, where the LORD walked and talked with the human pair.

In this scheme, the holy of holies represented Day One of the creation. 'Day One', rather than 'the first day', because that is what the text literally says: this day was outside time and matter, and so was not part of any temporal sequence. It was when the Holy One was One in his universe, according to Jewish tradition (Genesis Rabbah 3.8), and so was the state of undivided unity that was the presence of God before and beyond the visible creation. It was most holy. Now the distinction between holy and most holy was not simply a matter of degree. When a place or object or person was described as most holy, it meant 'imparting holiness'. The furnishings of the tabernacle were consecrated and became most holy: 'whatever touches them will become holy' (Exodus 30.29). Anyone who entered the holy of holies was transformed by the holiness and became a holy one, an angel. The high priests and the kings became angels.[2]

In Genesis, the scriptures for public reading, there is nothing about the angels and the powers of creation who were the fiery beings of the holy of holies. These were 'the matters within the veil' that were the exclusive preserve of the high priests, the only people allowed to enter (Numbers 18.7). We glimpse them elsewhere in the Old Testament, for

---

2   For detail see M. Barker. *The Great High Priest* (London and New York, 2003), pp. 103–45.

example in Psalm 104, which recounts the creation in the traditional order, but tells of the angel spirits and the fiery servants of God before describing the foundation of the visible earth (Psalm 104.3–5). The most familiar account of the invisible creation is in the Benedicite, where the whole creation, visible and invisible, is called to praise the LORD. We are over half way through the Canticle before the visible creation is mentioned; the angels and powers of creation, all the beings of Day One, are listed first. All these beings are a unity, since, beyond time and matter there are no means of division. They are the Glory, and Isaiah, once he had seen beyond the veil into the holy of holies, knew that the whole world was full of Glory (Isaiah 6.3).

The veil screened the divine glory from human eyes, and it symbolized matter. The four colours from which it was woven represented the four elements: red was fire, blue was air, purple was water (the dye came from a sea shell) and white was the earth (Josephus, *Jewish War* 5.212–3). Beyond matter was the invisible creation, the eternal presence of the pre-created light. Those who entered that state could look back into the world of time and matter and see the whole. The prophets saw all history – past, present and future. The prophet Habakkuk took his place in the holy of holies to look out and see what the LORD would reveal to him (Habakkuk 2.1). The psalmist went into the holy place where he learned the ultimate fate of the wicked (Psalm 73.17). This was the prophetic vision that held all things together. One of the wise sayings of Israel warned: 'Where there is no prophetic vision, the people unravel' (Proverbs 29.18, translating literally).

Those who saw beyond the veil glimpsed the light of the glory of the presence. This was the purpose of the thrice yearly pilgrimages to Jerusalem. 'Three times in the year shall all your men appear before the LORD' (Exodus 23.17; 34.23) is the usual translation, but the Hebrew actually says: 'Three times a year shall all your men see the face of the LORD'. It became the custom to read the letters differently.[3]

---

3 The meaning of a Hebrew word changes when the vowels are changed. Since the sacred text only had consonants, the vowels and therefore the meaning were supplied by the reader. In these texts, the crucial difference is between two forms of the verb: the *qal* form and the *niph'al* form, which look identical in the consonantal text but have different

The psalms show the original purpose of pilgrimage to the holy place: 'I shall behold [in a vision] thy face . . .' (Psalm 17.15); 'This is the generation of those who seek him, those who seek your face . . .' (Psalm 24.6 translating literally). 'Thy face O LORD do I seek. Hide not thy face from me' (Psalm 27.8–9). When the pilgrim saw the face, he described it as shining. 'Let thy face shine on thy servant' (Psalm 31.16); 'May God be gracious to us and bless us and make his face to shine upon us' (Psalm 67.1). There are many examples. Most familiar perhaps is the high priestly blessing: 'May the LORD make his face shine upon you and be gracious unto you [or the text may have been 'and give you life']. May the LORD lift up his face upon you and give you peace' (Numbers 6.25.25).

Once the pilgrim had glimpsed the vision, everything changed. Isaiah learned that the whole world was full of the Glory. At the Transfiguration, the disciples saw the shining presence of the LORD. This followed immediately on Jesus's promise that some of his disciples would live to see the Kingdom come in power (Mark 9.1). St John wrote: 'The Word became flesh and dwelt among us . . . And we beheld his glory . . .' (John 1.14). The word 'dwelt' here is literally 'tabernacled'. This was the older temple tradition, the glory appearing from the holy of holies. Seeing through the veil of matter to the radiance of the pre-created light was seeing the Kingdom, seeing the King. The imagery of the holy of holies became the imagery of the Kingdom in Christian discourse. Nicodemus was told that only those born from above, or reborn, could see and enter the Kingdom (John 3.3–7). When he prayed after the Last Supper, Jesus knew he was returning the Glory he shared with the Father before the world was made. He was returning to the state of the holy of holies (John 17.5). Jesus prayed that his followers would be One, 'so that the world may know that thou hast sent me' (John 17.23).

---

meanings. Exodus 23.17; 34.23 and Deuteronomy 16.16 can be read either as *qal* or *niph'al*, but in Exodus 34.24, and Isaiah1.12, the infinitive form of the verb can only be *qal* since the *niph'al* requires an additional consonant. The meaning therefore must be that the LORD appears, rather than that the people appear before the LORD.

Who Dwelt in the Holy of Holies?

The holy of holies was a twenty cubit cube lined with gold (1 Kings 6.20, about 30 metres). The account in 1 Kings is not entirely clear about the dimensions of the temple, nor is the account of the tabernacle clear as to the exact construction of the holy of holies. Given the age of the texts and their history, this is not surprising. There was to be a curtain or veil hung on four pillars to separate the holy place from the holy of holies (Exodus 26.31, 33), but we are not told how the pillars were placed: in a line, or at the four corners of a square. The veil is most often imagined as hung from the four pillars in a straight line, but this would have presented considerable practical difficulties, as the rabbis realized. We have to guess. The veil was a single piece of heavy linen and woollen fabric, and the high priest had to pass through it carrying a pan of burning incense or a bowl of blood. There must have been a way through. The account in the Mishnah – a compendium of Jewish lore and custom as it was in the time of Jesus – says there was a passageway a cubit wide 'between the two curtains', but the tradition is also clear that there was only one curtain. The 'two curtains' can only be understood as two parts of the curtain, in other words, an overlap at one point to allow the high priest to enter. The only possibility is that the veil was hung round four pillars set at the corners of a square (Mishnah Yoma 5.1). This is, of course, how the holy of holies is depicted in icons: a four pillared canopy with a curtain. The holy of holies was a house within a house.

The holy of holies is described in the temple visions of Enoch. Enoch is only mentioned once in the Old Testament (Genesis 5.18–24), but that gives no idea of his importance in Hebrew tradition. There is almost as much Enoch material among the Dead Sea Scrolls as there is of Isaiah, and this despite the very conservative character of the priestly community. Enochic ideas can be found throughout the New Testament, and until the Scrolls proved that Enoch was pre-Christian many thought it had been written by a Christian. Enoch experienced mystical ascents to the presence of God, and described how he entered a temple built of crystals and fire

(1 Enoch 14.9–11) and then saw a house within that house, in which was the divine throne (1 Enoch 14.15–18). This was the holy of holies, and most of the Enoch material is set in the holy of holies. Since access to the holy of holies was restricted to the high priesthood, information about the interior must have been high priestly tradition. In another account, Enoch says that the inner house was encircled by thousands of angels, clad in white and walking on fire (1 Enoch 71.1.8). Enoch's holy of holies had been free standing, a house within a house that represented the heart and the origin of creation.

A female figure lived in the inner house. She appears in the Book of Proverbs as the Creator's companion and describes herself and her place in the creation. She was brought forth before the beginnings of the earth, before the mountains and the springs had been made. In other word, she existed before the visible creation, and, in temple terms, this means she was in the holy of holies. Wisdom, for that is her name, was beside the Creator, holding all things together in harmony, as the Greek text puts it, and rejoicing always before the Creator (Proverbs 8.22–31). Her origin from the Creator is described in birthing language, which reminds us that gender imagery is difficult in the divine state. She was a child not a creature. Elsewhere in Proverbs she is described as the tree of life, who gives to her devotees long life, riches and honour (Proverbs 3.13–18); her name has a plural form – 'Wisdoms' – a sure sign of divinity, and in the preface to the book she appears as a divinity who has been rejected: 'Turn to my reproof and I will pour out my Spirit on you . . .' (Proverbs 1.23). Who was this rejected Lady who lived in the holy of holies and was represented by the tree of life?[4]

There are only a few clues, because of the problem of edited and excluded texts: first, the Book of Jeremiah describes a group of people who had fled from Jerusalem after the Babylonians had sacked the city. This was a generation after the time of King Josiah, and the refugees blamed him for the disaster. Jeremiah had been preaching that the disaster was due to their sins, but the refugees would have none of it. The reason, they said, was the changing of Jerusalem's

---

4   For more detail of the Lady in the Old Testament, Barker, op. cit., pp. 229–61.

religion: 'Since we left off burning incense to the Queen of Heaven and pouring out libations to her, we have lacked everything and been consumed by the sword and by famine' (Jeremiah 44.18). It would appear that King Josiah had banished a Lady known as the Queen of Heaven.

Second, the Enoch writings recorded that just before the temple had been burned by the Babylonians, the priests had 'lost their vision and godlessly forsaken Wisdom' (1 Enoch 93.8). There is no detail in 1 Enoch; the passage is a fragment of a stylized history, but Wisdom being forsaken when the Jerusalem priests changed their ways corresponds exactly to the time when the Queen of Heaven was abandoned.

Third, Ezekiel, who had been a priest in the first temple (Ezekiel 1.3) and was deported to Babylon, recorded his famous vision of the Glory of the LORD leaving the polluted temple. He saw the divine throne leaving the temple, hovering over the eastern gate (Ezekiel 10.19) and then passing over to the Mount of Olives (Ezekiel 11.23). What Ezekiel described was what a priest at that time imagined as the interior of the holy of holies. There is no other material as a context for these chapters, and so it is impossible to translate with confidence any word that has more than one meaning. Parts of the Hebrew text in the vision chapters (1, 10, 11) are opaque: singular and plural are interchanged, as are masculine and feminine forms. Ezekiel's vision describes two figures: one, a human form enthroned above the firmament of fearful ice, had the appearance of the likeness of the Glory of the LORD (Ezekiel 1.26–28). The other was, in effect, his throne. There was one wheel on the earth, constructed as a wheel within a wheel, which had rims or rings full of eyes or points of light, and the wheel surrounded a fourfold Living One, sometimes described as Living Ones, a plural of divinity. The Spirit of the Living One was in the wheels (Ezekiel 10.17). The sound of the Living One was like many waters, like the voice of El Shaddai (Ezekiel 1.24; 10.5).[5] The figure Ezekiel knew in the first temple was female, a compound

---

5   In the Hebrew, it is the voice, a masculine noun, that speaks, giving a masculine verb form. The gender of the owner of the voice is not known.

fourfold figure with fiery wings, surrounded by wheels within wheels which were full of points of light. The Lady was in some way the divine throne, the vehicle for the Glory of the LORD to appear in human form.

Jeremiah, Enoch and Ezekiel all record the departure of the Lady. The account in Kings 23 of the changes in Jerusalem, which has been accepted as the norm, was clearly influenced by the ideals of the temple reformers. The departure of the Lady is described as removing and destroying the Asherah, implying that her sacred tree symbol was an idolatrous object. King Josiah removed anything connected to the host of heaven, the angels; yet we know that 'LORD of Hosts' was an ancient title for Yahweh. Josiah also removed from the temple what we now read as 'the houses of the cult prostitutes'; but the same Hebrew letters can be read as 'the shrines of the holy ones'. In these houses, women had woven fine linen for the Lady, presumably as garments (2 Kings 23.4.7). Thus, hidden beneath the text we read today, there is a description of the Lady and her angels who were banished from the temple.

The banished Lady was known as 'the Queen of Heaven', 'Wisdom', and 'the Living One' – a name in Hebrew very similar to 'Eve'[6] – and one of her symbols was the tree of life. The rejection of the Lady is encoded in the familiar story of the fall, when the human pair chose the other tree. According to Genesis, when Adam was set in Eden, he was forbidden only one tree, the tree of the knowledge of good and evil. The fruit of the tree of life, the fruit of Wisdom, had been intended as his food. The serpent wanted things otherwise, and so the human pair chose the other tree and a different way of knowing. They chose the possibility of doing good or evil with their knowledge, rather than accepting the gift of divine Wisdom that came from the tree of life. Having made their choice they discovered the consequences. They became mortal and had to leave Eden to live in a world of thorns, thistles and dust. This is another way of telling the story in Enoch; that the priests rejected wisdom and then the temple was destroyed. The reversal of this situation is proclaimed in Revela-

---

6   Eve is *hawwah*, the Living One is *hayyah*.

tion 11.18. When the seventh angel blows the last trumpet to announce the Kingdom of the LORD coming to earth, it is time to destroy the destroyers of the earth. These are the agents of the great deceiver, and the next scene in the vision reveals Wisdom restored to the holy of holies: a woman clothed with the sun.

There are several places where the first five books of the Old Testament carry a meaning below the surface of the text. They were brought to their present form well into the period of the second temple, that is, about the fifth century BC. Ancient materials were reworked to preserve the history of Israel, but also to comment on it. Here is one relevant example. In Exodus there is the story of Moses at the burning bush, where he learns the new name for the God of Israel. In future, he was to be invoked as the LORD, Yahweh: 'This is my name for ever and thus I am to be invoked/remembered throughout all generations' (Exodus 3.15). In the time of the Patriarchs, we are told, the name of God had been different: 'I appeared to Abraham, to Isaac and to Jacob as El Shaddai, but by my name Yahweh I did not make myself known to them' (Exodus 6.3). Now the religion of the Patriarchs had involved sacred trees – Abraham planted a tree at Beersheba (Genesis 21.33) – sacred pillars that were anointed, as Jacob did at Bethel (Genesis 28.18), and altars set up wherever God had appeared, for example at Mamre (Genesis 13.18). King Josiah broke down the pillars and cut down the sacred trees, and closed down all shrines other than Jerusalem (2 Kings 23.8–9.14). In other words, what King Josiah destroyed sounds very like the religious practices of the Patriarchs. When Ezekiel heard the Living One leaving the temple, it sounded, he said, like the voice of El Shaddai (Ezekiel 1.24; 10.5).

Scholars realized some time ago that the sequence in Genesis and then Exodus – that is, the Patriarchs and then Moses – describes not a development in ancient history, but the process by which the religion of Moses came to prominence in the time of King Josiah at the expense of the religion of the Patriarchs.[7] The God of Israel had a different

---

7   See J. van Seters, 'The Religion of the Patriarchs in Genesis', *Biblica* 6(1) (1980), pp. 220–33.

name after the time of Moses, which probably means that there was a new name after the work of King Josiah. The voice from the burning bush told him that in future the divine name would be Yahweh. Before that time it had been El Shaddai. The most natural way to understand that name is not God Almighty, as appears in most translations, but the 'Deity with Breasts'. She spoke from the burning bush and told Moses that the God of Israel would in future have a different name. It seems – and at this distance we can say no more – that the older religion of Israel venerated a Lady, who was eclipsed but not forgotten after King Josiah's reformation. In Jerusalem and Judah, a huge number of small figurines have been found – a stylized female figure with prominent breasts and large eyes, and a body that is simply a pillar. None can be dated after the time of Josiah.[8]

The lost Lady was the Mother of the Son of God, the Mother of the LORD who was manifest in the Davidic king. There are many divine names in the Hebrew scriptures, but it was only after King Josiah's reform, and during the exile, that the strict monotheism we associate with the Old Testament was introduced, or possibly imposed. The different names had originally belonged to different divine beings.

The version of the Hebrew text of Deuteronomy 32.8 that was found among the Dead Sea Scrolls, pre-Christian in date, shows the early belief that God Most High, El Elyon, had many angel sons (later tradition says there were 70), to whom he allocated the nations of the earth.[9] He set Yahweh, the LORD, over Israel. Yahweh appeared in human form, for example to Abraham, and he was the King. The Davidic king in Jerusalem was his earthly manifestation. Isaiah, a prophet in Jerusalem before the time of Josiah, saw the King on his throne, Yahweh of Hosts (Isaiah 6.1–5), and the psalmist described processions of 'my God and King' into the temple (Psalm 68.24). The prophet saw the heavenly vision and the psalmist sang of the earthly manifestation in the human king.

---

8   R. Kletter, 'Between Archaeology and Theology. The Pillar Figurines from Judah and the Asherah', in A. Mazar (ed.) *Studies in the Archaeology of the Iron Age in Israel and Jordan* (Sheffield, 2001), pp. 179–216.

9   See P. S. Skehan, 'A Fragment of the Song of Moses (Deut 32) from Qumran', *Bulletin of the American Schools of Oriental Research* 136 (1954), pp. 12–14.

The early Christians knew the Old Testament had more than one divinity. St Paul, condemning idolatry and the many gods of his society, emphasized that the Christians knew one God, the Father, and one Lord, Jesus Christ (1 Corinthians 8.5–6). These were El Elyon and Yahweh. The appearances of Yahweh in the Old Testament had been pre-Incarnation appearances of the Son of God. St John wrote that Isaiah had seen his glory, and he meant the glory of Jesus (Isaiah 12.40–41). Sozomen, the fifth century church historian whose family lived in Palestine, described why Constantine built a great church at Mamre, which was not a Christian site. 'It was here that the Son of God appeared to Abraham, with two angels . . .' (Sozomen, *Church History* 2.4). This is the theophany recorded in Genesis 18, where Yahweh appeared to Abraham to promise him a son by Sarah. Jesus was recognized as the incarnation of Yahweh, the Son of God Most High. Gabriel announced to Mary that her son would be called the Son of the Most High (Luke 1.32).[10]

A few traces remain in our Old Testament of beliefs about the divine King as the Son of God Most High. It was an aspect of the monarchy that the later editors thought best forgotten and, unfortunately, many of the ancient texts are damaged and reconstruction is not easy. Psalm 110.3–4, for example, describes how a human being becomes a priest after the order of Melchizedek, how he is born in the glory of the holy ones: 'I have begotten you'. The glory of the holy ones was the holy of holies, and so the divine child was ritually born before the visible creation. The angels sang as the king was born: 'Unto us a child is born, unto us a son is given, and the government will be upon his shoulder . . .' (Isaiah 9.6). The Enoch tradition described how the Man entered the holy of holies and there was given the Name 'before the sun and the stars had been created' (1 Enoch 48.2–3), in other words, the Man had passed into the state beyond the material creation and there was given the Name Yahweh. St Paul wrote that God had highly exalted Jesus and given him the Name above all names (Philippians 2.9), and Jesus himself spoke of the

---

10   For detail see M. Barker *The Great Angel: A Study of Israel's Second God* (London, 1992).

glory he had shared with the Father before the world was made (John 17.5). Jesus thought and taught within this temple worldview.

A few traces also remain of the Mother of the King. Micah, an eighth century prophet, spoke of the ruler of Israel, the great shepherd who would 'come forth', whose origin was from ancient times. His mother is mentioned but rarely noticed: 'she who is in travail brings forth . . .' (Micah 5.4). Who was the unnamed mother of the great shepherd from ancient times? Micah's contemporary Isaiah also mentions the woman who would conceive and bear a son and name him Immanuel, 'God with us' (Isaiah 7.14). She was described as the '*almah*, a significant and known figure, remembered when the Hebrew text was translated into Greek as the Virgin, *parthenos*. Virgin had been a title of honour given to the great female deities of other cultures in the region, especially to Athirat, the mother of the sons of God in Ugaritic tradition. A complete scroll of Isaiah was found among the Dead Sea Scrolls, and it contains the only pre-Christian Hebrew text of the Immanuel passage. This section has not been found among the other fragments of Isaiah. Where our present text has 'Ask a sign of the LORD your God', this ancient text has 'Ask a sign *of the mother* of the LORD your God' a difference of only one letter. Now this may have been a reading unique to that one scroll – but it does mean that at least some people in the time of Jesus were familiar with the idea of the mother of Yahweh who brought forth Immanuel. It seems likely that this was the unnamed Lady in Micah, and the psalms suggest that she was in the holy of holies where the Immanuel was born.

Her rejected tree of life appears in the Enoch tradition as the tree banished from the temple, removed to a remote mountain that Enoch visited on one of his heavenly journeys. The tree was fragrant, and its leaves and blossoms never withered. It stood by the throne of God and would one day be transplanted to a holy place beside the house of the LORD, where its fruit would be life-giving food for the chosen ones (1 Enoch 25.4–5).[11] The Eucharistic symbolism is clear. Wisdom describes herself as this tree in the Wisdom of Jesus ben Sira.

---

11   The text of these verses is far from clear. This is the rendering of D. Olson, *Enoch: A New Translation* (North Richland Hills, 2004).

'She took root in Zion and spread herself like a cedar, a cypress, a palm, an olive and a plane. She gave forth the scent of spices and myrrh, and fed herself to her disciples' (ben Sira 24.13–22). Memories were long. The changes made in the time of King Josiah were remembered as a disaster, and people still longed for the true temple to be restored in the time of the Messiah. The traditional Jewish commentary on Numbers, compiled as late as the thirteenth century AD but preserving much older material, said that in the time of the Messiah, the ark would be restored to the temple together with the seven-branched lamp known as the menorah, the spirit, the fire and the cherubim. According to Exodus, the lampstand was made like a tree, with branches and flowers of almond work (whatever that meant: the word only occurs as a description of the lampstand (Exodus 25.31–36)). One of the meanings of the lamp was a tree. The spirit, the fire and the cherubim were all part of Ezekiel's vision of the Lady leaving the temple, and the ark was the symbol of the divine throne. One possible reconstruction would be that the future temple of the Messiah would restore the Lady and her symbols – the throne and the tree. In other words, the holiest place would no longer be empty. A variant of this tradition is found in the much earlier Babylonian Talmud, which says that at the time of Josiah certain things were hidden away: the ark and its contents – the manna and the high priestly rod that blossomed – and the anointing oil (b. Horayoth 12a). Since there was a menorah in the second temple, it cannot have been accepted as the true menorah. Perhaps it had acquired a new meaning, or even a new place in the temple. And for as long as the oil was missing, there could be no Messiah.

The holy anointing oil was extracted from the tree of life and was the sacrament of *theosis*, by which Wisdom gave herself to her children. They received her gifts of eternal life and knowledge. Thus St John could remind the Church: 'You have been anointed by the Holy One and you know all things' (1 John 2.20). The early Christians sang of this: 'He anointed me with his perfection, and I became as one of those who are near him (Odes of Solomon 36.6). In the Clementine Recognitions, St Peter told Clement the meaning of the word Christ: 'the Son of God . . . Him first God anointed with oil which was taken from the wood of the tree of life'. He went on to explain that Christ would anoint all the pious when they entered his Kingdom. 'In the present life, Aaron the first high priest, was anointed with a composition of chrism, which was made after the pattern of the spiritual chrism . . . If then this temporal grace, compounded by men, had such efficacy, consider how potent was that ointment extracted by God from a branch of the tree of life . . .' (Clementine Recognitions 1.45–46).

The Lady did return to the temple. In his vision, St John saw the ark restored to the holy of holies. Then he saw a Woman clothed with the sun about to give birth to her Son who was taken up to the throne of God (Revelation 11.19–12.6). Once the Son of Wisdom was enthroned, the deceiver of the whole world was thrown from heaven, and the great battle on earth began. In the final vision, St John saw the holy of holies restored to its original state: the heavenly throne, the tree of life and the river of life – all symbols of the Lady.

Two Postscripts

First, The Infancy Gospel of James, which tells the early life of Mary, describes her as Wisdom. She was a child in the temple and she danced before the LORD, just as Wisdom had been described in Proverbs 8. She left the holy place at puberty and worked as a weaver, making the new veil of the temple when she was pregnant with her Child. She was weaving the ancient symbol of matter, incarnation. In icons inspired by the Infancy Gospel, Mary is depicted in the holy of holies, which is a canopy with four pillars.

Second, there is the great church built in Jerusalem by the emperor Justinian and dedicated in 543 AD to the Holy Mother of God, the ever Virgin Mary. The building was exactly the same size as the temple Ezekiel saw in his vision, the new temple to which the Glory of the LORD would return (Ezekiel 43.1–5). It was built on the hill that was at that time believed to be the ancient Zion, and clearly meant that Justinian was restoring the temple. A few years before this, his armies had recaptured the temple treasures in Carthage. They had been taken to Rome after the fall of Jerusalem in 70 AD, and then to North Africa by the Vandals when they sacked Rome. The treasures in Rome had included the menorah, albeit the menorah of the second temple, which can still be seen on the arch of Titus, but sources for Justinian do not give details of which temple treasures were recovered. We cannot be certain that the menorah was among them, but it is likely. A Jew in Constantinople warned Justinian that if he kept the treasures, his capital would also be destroyed, and so the emperor sent everything to 'the temples of the Christians in Jerusalem' (Procopius, *Wars*, 4.9.55–7; 5.12.41). A contemporary Jewish text, the *Book of Zerubbabel*, contains dire warnings about an imminent war against the son of Satan, whose mother was a beautiful stone statue set up in a house of shame. This looks like a reference to the New Church. The son of Satan would set up Asherahs – the symbol of the Lady – all over the land, and people would come from all over the world to worship the statue, pour libations to her and burn incense.[12]

If the menorah had been sent to Jerusalem, and if the New Church dedicated to the Mother of God had been the new temple, it would explain why the anniversary of the church's dedication is still kept on 21 November as the Feast of the Entry of the Mother of God into the temple.

---

12   I published a full account of this as 'Justinian's New Church and the Entry of the Mother of God into the Temple', in *Sourozh: A Journal of Orthodox Life and Thought* 103 (2006), pp. 15–33.

Chapter 6

Prayer to the Virgin in the Late Middle Ages

Eamon Duffy

On 19 January 1511 the young King Henry VIII came to the shrine of the Virgin at Walsingham to give thanks for the birth, three weeks earlier on New Year's day, of a son, Henry Prince of Wales. He was the latest and, as it turned out, the last of a long line of English kings to come to the shrine. As he knelt in the Holy House he will have seen, close to the statue of the Virgin, the gilded image of his own father Henry VII and the line of royal devotees who came to kneel at the feet of the Virgin and to leave their gifts. The line stretched back through Henry VI in the 1440s to Henry II in 1226. Henry VIII would remain a pious client of our Lady of Walsingham for two thirds of his reign. When the Royal Commissioners came to destroy the shrine 26 years on, they would find there a candle still burning which was maintained at the cost of the king in perpetual intercession for the birth of a son and heir. In fact, Henry's first-born son died just over a month after that first visit, on 22 February. Had he survived, the medieval Holy House at Walsingham would almost certainly still be standing, and the history of England would have been unimaginably different.

Henry's gesture in travelling to give thanks to the Virgin was an absolutely characteristic medieval expression of devotion, for in the late Middle Ages almost anyone who prayed at all prayed to Mary. Her cult had begun to blossom in England, as everywhere else in Europe, in the twelfth century, and the growth of the fame of the shrine at Walsingham was itself a symptom and expression of her growing centrality in the Christian imagination, a centrality to which painting, architecture, book production and music all bore testimony. That cult showed itself at every level, not least in the addition of elaborate Lady chapels to most of the cathedrals and great churches of England from the late twelfth century onwards. In those often very lavish spaces an increasingly elaborate musical liturgy developed in honour of the Virgin, and the daily Lady mass became in many places the main sung service, requiring teams of singers, musicians and clerks to staff it. In the same way, in many parish and collegiate churches as well as in the cathedrals, by the fifteenth century the daily singing of an evening anthem to the Virgin, generally referred to as the *Salve*, though in fact a range of texts were used, had become a popular focus of lay piety. In late medieval London the wills of shopkeepers and merchants often contained bequests to provide clergy to assist at these musical services, and left money for singers and lights to beautify them. The *Salve* guild of St Magnus the Martyr, London Bridge, employed chaplains and clerks to sing the Lady Mass and the antiphon to the Blessed Virgin Mary (usually sung each evening, but sometimes after the Lady Mass). In other churches, the *Salve* and other Marian anthems were sung only on certain weekday evenings – Friday and Saturday being the favourites. And the spread of musical services in honour of the Virgin was not confined to cathedrals and city churches. In fifteenth century North Yorkshire, for example, 'Our Lady Service or Guild' was one of seven such guilds in Topcliffe and was fairly typical of the 'services' maintained by parishioners in many places to augment the worship of their churches, in this case the votive offices and mass of the Blessed Virgin Mary. The guild chaplain was required not only 'to say masse and to pray for the prosperytie of the parochienns, lyvyng, and for the soules of them departed' but also 'to kepe the queyer with .vj. chyldren all haly and festyvall days; which .vj. chyldren the same incumbent is bounde to teche to syng, and to fynde song bokes for the servyce ther'. In 1522, the Lincolnshire merchant John Robinson left money to the guild of our Lady in Boston to provide 'two honest priests' skilled both in plainsong and polyphony to enhance the services of the guild in honour of our Lady.

This elaboration of the services devoted to the Virgin – her Mass, her offices and her anthems – was perhaps most famously expressed in the foundation of Eton College in 1440, where 70 poor scholars were to be educated and where a team of ten priest Fellows, ten chaplains, ten clerks and 16 choristers would maintain an elaborate round of musical services in honour of the Virgin. Eton rapidly became the centre of a blossoming cult of the Virgin, with a major pilgrimage there on the feast of the Assumption each year (the college organized a fair to coincide with the pilgrimage, which lasted for six days). Two astonishing monuments to this flourishing fifteenth-century cult of the Virgin at Eton survive to this day. One is the remarkable set of wall paintings commissioned for the north wall of the new college chapel in 1480, painted in the latest Flemish style and depicting the miracles of the Virgin Mary. Incidentally, by the 1480s this was rather an old-fashioned choice of subject for a Marian cycle. Miracles of the Virgin had been a popular theme in thirteenth- and fourteenth-century Books of Hours, and a magnificent sculptured cycle of the miracles of the Virgin was the chief decoration of the Lady Chapel at Ely. But by the Tudor period a more scriptural emphasis was fashionable, and when the new windows at Eton's sister-foundation at King's College were installed a generation later, they would illustrate the life of the Virgin and of her son Jesus, and not her posthumous miracles. All the same, the Eton miracle cycle was popular and impressive enough to be imitated in the Lady Chapel at Winchester Cathedral *c.* 1500. The Eton miracle-cycle pictures are among the best preserved paintings of the English late Middle Ages. But the most precious survival of the cult of the Virgin from Eton is the great choir-book compiled between 1490 and 1502. The book, one of only a handful of extant archives of fifteenth-century English choral music and far and away the fullest of them, originally contained Mass, office and motet settings in honour of the Virgin by 24 different composers. It is now damaged and incomplete, (98 pages or one third of the total is missing), but even so it contains nine different settings of the *Magnificat* for use at Vespers, (out of an original fifteen) and it also contained 40 motets and votive antiphons in honour of Mary. Those that survive include settings of some of the most famous hymns and anthems in her honour, from the *Salve Regina* to the *Stabat Mater*, as well as settings of other texts immensely popular then but hardly known at all now, like the multiple settings of the anthem *Stella Coeli Extirpavit*, which invokes the Virgin as protectress against the plague.

The Eton music and paintings were created for a royal foundation: this was Marian piety for an educational and social elite. But the cult of Mary stretched all the way down the social scale, and the late Middle Ages saw the emergence of the most popular of all devotions to the Virgin, one that is still alive and well today, for the most familiar fifteenth-century prayer to the Virgin is the rosary. Strings of beads or knots had been used for counting repetitious prayers for centuries, but it was not until quite late on in the Middle Ages that the prayer we know as the rosary took its familiar form. Early medieval prayer-beads were known as Paternosters, and as that suggests, were used for counting multiple recitations of the Our Father. It was common to repeat prayers in multiples of 50 or 150, in imitation of the monastic recitation of the 150 psalms of the psalter, and circular strings of beads were sometimes called 'psalters'. Multiple repetitions of the Hail Mary could not happen, of course, until the Hail Mary itself emerged as a separate prayer, and that seems not to have occurred until the twelfth century. Till the late sixteenth century the Hail Mary was not in fact a prayer at all, strictly speaking, but a salutation or greeting, consisting of the opening words of the Angel Gabriel to Mary at the Annunciation, and some of the words of Elizabeth to Mary at the Visitation – 'Hail Mary full of grace, the Lord is with thee' and 'Blessed art thou amongst women, and blessed is the fruit of thy womb'. The addition of the name Jesus, and the whole of the second half of the modern Hail Mary – 'Holy Mary Mother of God pray for us Sinners now and at the hour of our death', was not added until the sixteenth century and did not become a routine part of the prayer until 1568. The words of the first half of the Hail Mary, forming the whole of the prayer throughout the later Middle Ages, had so far as we know first been brought together in the late sixth century in the offertory anthem for the mass for the fourth Sunday in Advent. They did not float free as a separate prayer, recited by lay people, until the emergence in the eleventh century of the set of devotions known as the Little Hours of Virgin Mary.

This was a sort of mini-breviary, arranged like the breviary round the eight monastic Hours of prayer from Matins and Lauds to Vespers and Compline, and drawing on some of the most beautiful psalms in the psalter . Round these were grouped hymns, prayers and antiphons in honour of the Virgin. Because it was relatively short, and did not change much with the changing liturgical seasons, the Little Hours became immensely popular with well-to-do literate lay people, women as much as – or even more than – men; by the end of the Middle Ages, Books of Hours would be the most popular of all books. The most often recurring text throughout the Little Hours was the Angel's greeting, 'Ave Maria, Gratia Plena', used as an antiphon to top and tail the psalms, and it seems to have been the prominence given to this salutation in the Hours of the Virgin that set lay people using these words as a staple of daily prayer even when they were not using the book. Inevitably, people who could not read began to use multiples of this short Hail Mary – 50, 100, 150, in place of the psalms, and naturally the chaplets of psalters of Paternoster beads already in use to count Paternosters and other prayers were now used to count Hail Marys. In the course of the fourteenth and early fifteenth centuries a lot of different people had the idea of attaching texts, stories or verses relating incidents from the life and passion of Jesus to these prayers for people to meditate on while they recited the words of the Hail Mary as a sort of mantra. To begin with, in order to use any of these schemes you would have needed a book or sheet of paper in front of you, because there was often a single verse of scripture, or a verse of a rhyme or hymn, for every single Hail Mary so no-one could have memorised them all, and of course they would have been no good at all to the majority of the population who were illiterate. But in the 1470s and 1480s Friars of the Dominican Observant Movement (to which Savanorola belonged), anxious to promote a biblical prayer-life among ordinary people, simplified these schemes down to the familiar fifteen joyful, sorrowful and glorious mysteries and commissioned printed broadsheets, often arranged like chaplets of roses in three groups of five depicting the mysteries, often without any text at all. These pictures helped make the mysteries easy to remember, and the rosary now took off as the most popular of all schemes of prayer. Its spread was helped by the establishment of Dominican rosary confraternities, offering well-publicized indulgences and other spiritual benefits to anyone who joined them.

The Observant Movement was slow to catch on in England, and there is not much evidence of the spread of rosary confraternities here. But even so, in England as elsewhere, the rosary was a universal prayer. Everybody, rich or poor, said it, and everybody who was anybody owned a rosary. Rosaries suited all pockets, as well as all spiritual abilities. They might be as simple as ten dried beans on a piece of string, or they might be an elaborate chain strung with coral or amber, ivory or ebony, and images of them are everywhere in representations of late medieval and early Tudor people. Making and selling rosaries became big business, and in fifteenth-century London the workshops of the manufacturers of rosary beads clustered together in the streets to the north and west of St Paul's Cathedral, and street names there still commemorate the trade: Paternoster Row, Ave Maria Lane.

The Hail Mary was, of course, said in smaller numbers than the ten or 50 of the rosary. Though the Angelus as we have it had not yet been invented, the custom was spreading of reciting three Hail Marys in honour of the Incarnation at the ringing of a bell called the Ave Bell, at six o'clock in the morning, at noon, and at nine in the evening. Queen Elizabeth of York, Henry VII's wife, petitioned the Pope for an indulgence of 300 days for the recitation of this form of the Angelus, and that papal grant was augmented in 1492 by other local indulgences of 40 days for each time of recitation, granted by the Archbishops of Canterbury and York and nine other bishops, showing that repeating Hail Marys was something that royalty and the hierarchy were just as keen to promote as any village priest.

The rosary grew out of the Book of Hours and became in effect a sort of Book of Hours for those who could not read. But more and more people, women included, *could* read in the later Middle Ages, and the use of the Book of Hours was very widespread, especially once printing made such books widely and cheaply available. Books of Hours were scriptural prayer books, focused on the Incarnation,

Mary's part in the Incarnation, and all that flowed from it. They were also crammed, of course, with non-biblical material – suffrages to and images of the saints, litanies, indulgenced prayers to the wounds of Jesus, to the Blessed Sacrament, as well as to the Virgin Mary. But overwhelmingly the prayers of the Hours were drawn from the psalter, and the illustrations in most of those books which had any illustrations at all were predominantly scenes from the Bible depicting the Infancy of Jesus, or the incidents of his Passion. The core of the book was the Little Office of the Virgin, with its constant refrain of 'Ave Maria Gratia Plena', the greeting of the Angel Gabriel. The hymns and lessons of the Hours returned again and again to the moment at which God took human flesh in the womb of the Virgin at the Annunciation. Like the pictures which often preceded each of the Hours, they formed in effect a prolonged meditation on the mystery of the Incarnation, while the psalms these offices contained included many of the most tender and beautiful prayers of the psalter – 'I will lift up mine eyes to the Mountains'; 'I was glad when I heard them say'; 'God be merciful unto us and bless us'; 'When the Lord turned again the captivity of Sion'. The Hours also included some of the most beautiful and resonant of Marian prayers – antiphons like the Salve Regina, hymns like the exquisite Ave Maris Stella. These texts would have been familiar to any devout literate person wanting to say their prayers devoutly, and naturally they often provided the words which composers set to music for the *Salve* services, which were so popular with lay people. These prayers to Mary from the Book of Hours inspired some of the most sublime music ever written in England.

The core of Marian devotion in the Book of Hours focused on the Incarnation. But the range of prayers to and about Mary was very wide. Many of the hymns contained in these books celebrated in particular her joys and her sorrows. One of the most popular was the hymn *Gaude Virgo Mater Christ*:

> Rejoice, O Virgin, Mother of Christ
> Who conceived through the ear
> At Gabriel's announcement

Rejoice, for filled with the Godhead
You gave birth without pain
With the Lily of purity
Rejoice, because of him who was born of you
And whose death you mourned
The Resurrection shines forth.
Rejoice at the ascension of Christ,
Into the heavens while you looked on
Carried upwards by his own power.
Rejoice because you ascend there after him
And that you have there great honour
In the palace of high heaven.
Where may it be granted to us
To enjoy the fruit of your womb
In unending rejoicing.

These Latin prayers and hymns on Mary's joys were immensely popular: they were frequently set by composers and lines from them, in Latin, were woven into the English devotional poems and carols which were multiplying throughout the fourteenth and fifteenth centuries. Richard Hill, a London grocer who copied devotional texts into his commonplace book in the early sixteenth century, includes one long devotional poem which is an expanded version of the *Gaude Virgo Mater Christi*. The first verse – with an excruciating rhyme for *Gabrielis Nuncio* – is as follows:

Gaude Maria, Christe's Mother!
Mary mild, of thee I mean:
Thou bare my Lord, thou bare my brother,
Thou bare a lovely child and clean.
Thou stoodest full still without blyn,
When in thy ear that errand was done-so:
Thy gracious God the light within,
Gabrielis Nuncio.

The Joys of Mary provided one of the recurrent themes of Marian piety, but her Sorrows were equally central. By the end of the Middle Ages many Books of Hours included the *Stabat Mater*, a poem which dwelt on the tears and heartbreak of the Virgin under the Cross as she watches her son die, intended to evoke tears of sorrow from the penitent for the sins that had crucified him. The *Stabat Mater* is a text constantly set by medieval and early Tudor composers, a sure sign of its wide popularity, and prayers evoking the sorrows of Mary recur again and again in the devotions of the period. The fifteenth century was captivated by the power of Mary's sorrow, the grief of the mother lamenting her dead child, which resonated with men and women for whom such bereavements were very common. This is the era in which the image of the Pieta, Our Lady of Pity, caught the lay religious imagination. Statues of the Pieta appeared in many churches, and in the county of Kent on the eve of the Reformation the most popular location for burial was in the church, near the statue of the Pieta. Images of the Pieta were often reproduced in prayer-books and as separate devotional prints, and poems and prayers evoking Mary's sorrow as she cradles the dead Christ multiplied. We have a vivid eye-witness account of a pious East Anglian housewife's first encounter with the Pieta. Margery Kempe saw one in a Norwich church early in the fifteenth century and 'through the beholding of that pity her mind was all wholly occupied in the Passion of our Lord Jesus Christ and in the compassion of our Lady St Mary, by which she was compelled to cry full loud and weep full sore, as though she should have died. Then came to her a priest, saying, "Damsel, Jesus is dead long since". When her crying was ceased, she said to the priest, "Sir, his death is as fresh to me as though he had died this day, and so I think it ought to be to you, and to all Christian people.'

The Joys and the Sorrows might be prayed together. Books of Hours almost invariably included a long Latin prayer to the Virgin commemorating her Joys and her Sorrows together, which began *Obsecro te, Domina sancta Maria Mater Dei.* It is too long to translate in its entirety here, but it is remarkable in the first place for the beautiful series of titles by which it invokes the Virgin – a sort of Litany of the Virgin: 'I implore you, holy Lady, Mother of God full of tender love, daughter of the High King, mother most glorious, mother of orphans, consolation of the desolate, right road for those who go astray, health and hope of all who hope in thee. Virgin before child-birth, virgin in childbirth, virgin after childbirth. Fountain of mercy, fountain of health and grace, fountain of tenderness and joy, foun-tain of consolation and gentleness'. The prayer then goes on to invoke Mary's help through the joy of the Incarnation. 'By that holy and inestimable joy which exalted your spirit in that hour when, through the Archangel Gabriel the Son of God was announced to you and conceived within you. And by the holy and inestimable tender care grace, mercy, love and humility by which the Son of God descended to take human flesh in your most venerable womb . . . And by those most holy fifteen joys which you had from Our Lord Jesus Christ.' The prayer then turns to invoke Mary by her sorrows:

> By that great and holy compassion and most bitter sorrow of heart which you had when Our Lord Jesus Christ was stripped naked before the Cross, and you saw him raised and hanging there, crucified, wounded, thirsting with bitter gall set before him, when you heard him cry out and saw him dying. And by your Son's Five Wounds, and the sorrow you had to see him wounded. And by the fountain of his Blood, and all his passion, and by all the sorrows of your heart, and by the fountains of your tears.

The drift towards the creation of a Marian litany which can be detected in that prayer is present also in some of the pictures illustrating printed Books of Hours from the late fifteenth century. Representations of the Virgin surrounded by emblems of the titles given to her in patristic and medieval theology and piety anticipate the titles of the Litany of Loretto. The Parisian publisher François Regnault, who dominated the market for Books of Hours in England during the reign of Henry VIII, regularly included such pictures which he used on the title page of one of his best-selling series, and the labels on the emblems make up a litany – Star of the Sea, Tower of David, Mirror without spot, garden enclosed, cedar of Lebanon, Gate of Heaven, and so on. There were similar pictures of the Virgin's mother, St Anne, with the Virgin in her womb, an image encapsulating the doctrine of the Immaculate Conception.

Thus far I have emphasized aspects of late medieval Marian piety which we can readily understand and which would not seem strange to a modern Roman Catholic or Anglo-Catholic. But it is also worth emphasizing that Marian piety might take rather less familiar forms. Fifteenth-century pilgrimage, for example, was more complicated than it might perhaps first appear. Devotion to the Virgin was focused almost everywhere on favoured images of Mary. Walsingham was the greatest of these, but even in East Anglia there were other important Marian shrines. Our Lady of Woolpit in Suffolk was an image in a chapel on the north side of Woolpit church. By the early thirteenth century the offerings of pilgrims were significant enough for Bury Abbey to demand a share: by 1286 a fair had sprung up, held on the main pilgrimage day, 8 September, the feast of the Nativity of the Virgin. By the fifteenth century local people were lavishing gifts on the shrine, like the diamond ring bequeathed by Dame Elizabeth Andrews of Baylham in 1473, one of a pair, the other of which went to Our Lady of Walsingham, or the 'pair of beads of thrice sixty garnished with silver and three gold rings set thereto, with a cross and heart of silver' offered to the shrine by Robert Reydon of Creeting in 1505, on condition that they remained always round the neck of the image of Our Lady of Woolpit. From the 1450s to the late 1520s local wills from many of the surrounding villages and towns – Thorndon, Thurston, Otley, Gislingham, Wetheringsett, Kelsale, Fornham – made arrangements for pilgrimages on behalf of the dead to our Lady of Woolpit, and the shrine had clearly become a focus of regional identity. Monarchs or their wives on progresses round the regions consolidated local goodwill by making a point of devout attendance at the major local shrines. John, Lord Howard of Stoke by Nayland, future Duke of Norfolk, made several benefactions of money, lights and silver-gilt votive images to our Lady of Woolpit in the early 1480s, and Woolpit was one of the five East Anglian shrines (alongside Our Lady of Walsingham, Ipswich, Sudbury and Stoke by Clare) to which Queen Elizabeth of York, the same who had procured the Angelus, sent a pilgrim to pray for her in Lent 1502. But the shrine might also be a place of punishment by shame. In 1499 a group of parishioners from the village of Great Ashfield, four miles from Woolpit, were found guilty of magical practices. They were required to perform public penance not only in their parish church, but at Norwich Cathedral, Bury St Edmund's market-place, and during the procession at the shrine of Our Lady of Woolpit, where they were required to offer candles to the image of St Mary in the chapel.

If pilgrimage as punishment is an unexpected idea, prayers too might be used in ways disconcerting to modern Christians. Many of the prayers to the Virgin found in Books of Hours and other devotional collections are prefaced by rubrics attaching not only spectacular indulgences to their use, but often miraculous promises: the devout user will not die a sudden death, or will be protected on their travels, or the Virgin will appear to them on their deathbed to take them to heaven. There is a good example of such a prayer copied into a manuscript Book of Hours now in the Cambridge University Library (CUL Ii 6 2). The book was produced in the Netherlands for the English market in the early fifteenth century. It was bought by a Suffolk family, and was used in East Anglia for at least two generations. Eventually it was sold or given away and was acquired by the Roberts family, well-to-do gentry from Neasden in Middlesex. They copied many additional prayers into the book, and one of these prayers is an elaborate ten-day devotion which involved the recitation of a thousand Hail Marys. Here is what the book says about it:

Ye shall say M [a thousand] tyme Ave Maria [Hail Mary] and ye shall sey them in X days, that is every day a hundreth, and ye shall say them standyn and goyng and knelyng or syttynge and ye shall have a certen almys in your hande while ye make your prayer, and after, say thys orison or prayer that followeth.

O Adonai, Lord, great and wonderful God, who gave the salvation of human kind into the hands of the most glorious Virgin, your Mother Mary: through her womb and merits, and through that most holy body which you took from her, in your goodness hear my prayers and fulfil my desires for [my] good, to the praise and glory of your

*name. Liberate me from every tribulation and assailant, and from all
the snares of my enemies who seek to harm me, and from lying lips
and sharpened tongues, and change all my tribulation into rejoicing
and gladness. Amen.*

And when ye have seide thys orison kysse your almos, and after,
geve it to a pore man or woman in honour of that blyssed joy that
seynt Gabryel greeted our Lady [with], and for what thyng ye do
thys ten days together, without doubt ye shall have that thynge ye
pray for lawfully, with Goddes Grace.

[Added in English in a later hand (1553), 'I used this prayer well
ten days, Edmund Roberts *inquit* (*says*)'.]

Other versions of this thousand Aves charm are to be found in a
number of surviving fifteenth-century Books of Hours. Like so many
of the prayers I have been considering, the charm focuses on the
story of the Annunciation, when the Angel Gabriel greeted Mary, the
precise moment when Christ took human flesh and became a child
in the Virgin's womb. It's a devotion which turned on a mixture of
good intentions, multiple repetition, and the giving of money: the
devotee is to recite a 100 Hail Marys (the equivalent of two rosaries)
every day – the prayers can be recited while the devotee goes about
their ordinary business, 'standing, going, kneeling or sitting', but is
linked to the late medieval preoccupation with the works of mercy
listed by Christ in the parable of the sheep and the goats (Matthew
25) as a means of salvation. The success of the prayer is said to
depend on its being accompanied by the relief of the poor, in honour
of the Annunciation. But this edifying link is made in a quasi-magical
way, which the church authorities would certainly have condemned
– holding money in the hand while the thousand Aves are recited,
then kissing it before handing it to the poor recipient. To the thousand Aves is added a Latin prayer which emphasizes the centrality in
the salvation of mankind of the physical reality of the Incarnation at
the Annunciation. Christ is invoked by his mother's womb and by the
flesh he himself took on in that womb. That flesh is declared to
protect the user of the prayer especially from their enemies. Prayers

against enemies – corporeal and incorporeal – were a very prominent feature of late medieval piety. Characteristically, the English instructions attached to the prayer display some awareness of the precarious line being trodden between 'legitimate' prayer and forbidden 'magic': success is guaranteed if the prayer is rightly used (a guarantee theologians rejected as magical), but that guarantee is softened by the reference to praying 'lawfully, with God's grace'. Another version of this charm included in a Book of Hours now in Ushaw College Durham declares that 'withoutttyn doute ye may noght fayle of that ye pray for and your desire be resonabyll'.

As I hope all this has suggested, prayer to the Virgin in late medieval England was very varied, and appealed to an enormously wide social spectrum. On one end of that spectrum were poor and illiterate people whose devotions perhaps never went much beyond reciting Hail Marys, with or without beads to help them count. At the other, there were the sophisticated glories of the Wilton Diptych and the exquisite and elaborate webs of music in Mary's honour woven by composers such as John Dunstaple, John Browne and William Cornysh. People prayed to Mary using illuminated books worth a king's ransom, or by lighting a candle in front of the statue in their parish church, or by saying five Hail Marys on their fingers. In a religion dominated by men, her cult fostered gentleness and tenderness, and made a place for homely things to which ordinary men and women could relate – for the mysteries of birth and nurture, for hope and for tears. And it was a cult which linked rich and poor: the wealthy might pray from Latin books, but they also prayed on strings of beads; kings came on foot to her shrines, and it was a queen of England that persuaded the pope to give Englishmen and women an indulgence for praying at the Angelus-bell.

And it was a king, in the end, who called a halt to her cult. The prior and monks of Walsingham surrendered their priory and the shrine to the Crown in August 1538, and all over England pilgrimages came to an end. For a little while longer Englishmen and women would pray to the Virgin, but the reformers were increasingly hostile to a cult which they thought robbed the Virgin's son of his due honour. With the accession of King Edward VI, even rosary beads would be forbidden, and after the death of Edward's Catholic sister Mary and a brief Catholic revival, those prohibitions would deepen. The Lady chapels were stripped of their imagery and became redundant space, the books of music dedicated to her were dismembered and burned or used to wrap butter and meat. Christianity, for the Protestant English, became a male religion.

Suggestions for Further Reading

For the earliest history of the cult of the Virgin in England: Mary Clayton, *The Cult of the Virgin Mary in Anglo-Saxon England.* (Cambridge, 1990). For its development in thirteenth- and fourteenth-century England, especially in the liturgy, see the essays by Nigel Morgan, 'Texts and Images of Marian Devotion', in W. M. Ormrud (ed.) *England in the Thirteenth Century* (Stamford, 1991), pp. 69–103, and N. Rogers (ed.) *England in the Fourteenth Century* (Stamford, 1993), pp. 34–57. For pilgrimage to Walsingham in the Middle Ages, J. C. Dickinson, *The Shrine of Our Lady of Walsingham* (Cambridge, 1956). For Our Lady of Woolpit, C. Paine, 'The Chapel and Image of Our Lady of Woolpit', *Proceedings of the Suffolk Institute of Archaeology* (38), 1996, pp. 8–12.

The cycle of pictures on the miracles of the Virgin at Eton is edited in M. R. James, *Eton College Chapel, the Wall-Paintings* (London, 1923). For the Eton Choir Book, Magnus Williamson, 'The Eton Choir-Book: Collegiate Music-Making in the reign of Henry VII', in Benjamin Thompson (ed.) *The Reign of Henry VII* (Stamford, 1995), pp. 213–28, and for modern recordings from the book, the same author's 'The Recording History of the Eton Choirbook', *Early Music* XXV (2), pp. 291–5. Harry Christophers and The Sixteen have recently issued a series of five CDs on the CORO label including most of the finest anthems and hymns to the Virgin from the Eton book. For parish and guild music-making and the *Salve*, Magnus Williamson, 'Liturgical Music in the Late Medieval English Parish', in Clive Burgess and Eamon Duffy (eds) *The Parish in Late Medieval England* (Stamford, 2006), pp. 177–242.

For prayer to the Virgin and the Book of Hours, Eamon Duffy, *The Stripping of the Altars* (New Haven and London, 1992), chapter 7, and *Marking the Hours: English People and Their Prayers 1240–1570* (New Haven and London, 2006).

For the Rosary, the best general treatment is now Anne Winston-Allen, *Stories of the Rose: The Making of the Rosary in the Middle Ages* (University Park, PA, 1997). For the beads themselves, the quirkier *Rose-Garden Game: A Tradition of Beads and Flowers* by Eithne Wilkins (London, 1969) is still worth consulting, and see also Ronald Lightbown, *Medieval European Jewellery* (London, 1992). On the evolution of the Hail Mary, the best discussion in English is still Herbert Thurston, *Familiar Prayers. Their Origin and History* (London, 1953).

For images of the Virgin, Richard Marks, *Image and Devotion in Late Medieval England* (London, 2004).

Seven Cairns[1] in the Creation of Sacred Space in the City

Ann Morisy

It can be tedious to start by defining one's terms, but this subject brings up two ideas that, if not exactly contentious, are certainly open to the challenge: 'What do you mean by urban or city?' and 'What do you mean by sacred?' I do not propose to offer definitions, simply to acknowledge that what I offer will be partial – and idiosyncratic.

In reflecting on this theme I found myself adapting the often used phrase accorded to Jesus in the gospels: 'Let those with ears hear'. Or rather, in this case, 'Let those with the inclination to sense the sacred do so'. Whilst all of us have the capacity to sense the holy, not everyone has the inclination to do so. Furthermore, there is a hazard: the capacity to perceive or sense the holy, or the sacred, if not fostered and developed, can atrophy. Our context today is one which risks such atrophy, because our perceptions are so often earthbound and mundane.

Increasingly Earthbound?

As a child I remember sitting alongside my Dad to chortle at *Morecambe and Wise* on the TV. Zany and homely comedy was the order of the day. Thirty years later, judging by the TV schedule for Christmas Day, that same experience of child/adult bonding will be focused around *Little Britain*. I laugh as much as anyone at the antics of

---

1 A cairn is a small pyramid of stones placed along the route to the mountain top to help show the way to the summit.

David Walliams and Matt Lucas, but I hesitate to share with you what I laugh at. Whilst *Little Britain* puts the hypocrisy of many aspects of modern life under a powerful spotlight, it does so by indulging in the earthiest and most base processes. *Little Britain* quite literally rubs our noses in our creaturely outpourings. If TV schedules are anything to judge by, we seem increasingly gripped by crudity and creatureliness – just consider programmes such as *Shameless, You Are What You Eat, The Green Room* and countless detective stories that gravitate around the postmortem slab.

Our fixation with materialism – 'stuff' in modern parlance – doesn't help either. Rubem Alves, writing in 1969, suggested that 'technology creates a false man (*sic*), a man who learns how to find happiness in what is given to him by the system. His soul is created as the image of what he can have'.[2] In cultures that are affluent, highly individualistic and dominated by micro-technology, the loss of any sense of the holy is almost inevitable. So those larger that life characters that populate *Little Britain* are aeons away from being inclined to sense the holy or the sacred. Why? Because they are so self-engrossed that they have little capacity to embrace the self-forgetfulness that is essential to the perception of the sacred. Urban man and woman, preoccupied as we are with the earthy and material – and with ourselves – have all but truncated the experience of life by the excision of the sacred in it. Encouraging people to sense the holy in life is to subvert the everyday habits and inclinations of increasingly earthbound people: to create sacred space therefore is to make a radical offering.

It is indeed a radical act to wish to create a sense of the sacred and holy in the midst of the urban. It is that of which we are most needful – and to which we are most resistant. Even for people of faith, there may be resistance. Little though one may like this, it is possible for the felt presence of God to be obliterated by other 'religious' priorities. Ronald Rolheiser comments that: 'Rather God is experienced and related to us as a religion, a church, a moral philosophy, a guide for private virtue, an imperative for justice, or a nostalgia for proper

---

2   R. M. Alves, *A Theology of Human Hope* (Washington, 1969), p. 23.

propriety'; and again that God and religion are, like the royal family in England: '. . . a symbolic anchor for a certain way of life . . .'[3] Too easily the sense of the holy or the sacred can evaporate from everyday awareness.

Cairn One: Encouraging Self-forgetfulness

In part our resistance has its roots in our self-preoccupation, because self-forgetfulness is an essential part of the process of responding to the holy. Hence the first step in the therapeutic journey to restore the human right to be more than just a creature involves fostering the experience of self-forgetfulness. This is the first cairn or way marker on the journey to create sacred space. Therefore art, creativity and fun, all of which have the potential to promote a degree of self-forgetfulness, need to be part of our repertoire of community involvement if we are to create sacred space for metropolitan man and woman.

Art – both in the doing, and in the looking and seeing – has the capacity so to claim our attention that noisy, preened and overweening egos can, for the moment, be stilled and forgotten. But more than this, Herbert Marcuse, in his pioneering book *One Dimensional Man*, makes the point that art has the capacity to make us discontented with the taken-for-granted world.[4] Art can lift us out of our creatureliness and earthiness and remind us of our potential for something more profound. In a context where those who dwell in the city have become fixated on the material and earthbound, the arts become part of the dynamics of redemption. Art, whether painting, singing, dancing or sculpting, and whether in the doing or the encountering, has the capacity to lift our eyes and stir our hearts, prompting awareness of those parts of metropolitan man and woman that have been left unfulfilled.

The apostle Paul writes to the Romans (8.26) that there are

---

3   R. Rolheiser, *The Shattered Lantern* (New York, 1997), p. 16.
4   H. Marcuse, *One Dimensional Man: Studies in the Ideology of Advanced Industrial Society* (Boston, 1964 (repr. London, 1991)), esp. pp. 228–46.

groanings of the heart that cannot be put into words or grasped by rationality alone.[5] The arts, whether music, painting or sculpture, may be close cousins of prayer in their capacity to give expression to such longings and in their capacity 'to take our breath away'; they can consequently allow the sense of the hallowed or sacred to flow. On occasion, to the extent of flowing in the direction of love and intimacy, these dynamics prefigure or prepare metropolitan men and women for the gracious offer of God to be present to his sons and daughters.

Cairn Two: Fostering a Sense of Timelessness

The second cairn on the journey to enable city dwellers to respond to the holy is playfulness in defiance of time. First, however, a caution is required. Whilst play is an authentic expression of humanity, Moltmann cautions that 'if on earth everything turns into play, nothing will be play . . . play should liberate, not tranquilise or anesthetise'.[6] Play, despite its capacity to lift us out of self-absorption, is not guaranteed to lead to a redemptive end – especially since the advent of Xboxes and Game Boys. It may be quite possible to 'entertain ourselves to death', to quote the title of Neil Postman's prophetic book,[7] as the challenge of participating gets neglected in favour of long sessions of thumb gymnastics.

Play has traditionally involved self-forgetfulness in the context of *being with* others. The experience of play can be an experience of timelessness and joyfulness that can never be created consciously. It comes upon each of us signifying the grace which enfolds our world and our being. In gaining confidence in these gracious dynamics that defy time, allowing the sloughing off of years to reveal the 'child within' that never grows old, is to proclaim the validity and reality of eternity. In playfulness we also find laughter and as Peter Berger suggests, play and laughter can be a 'rumour of angels'.[8]

---

5   Romans 8.26: 'We do not know what we ought to pray for, but the Spirit himself intercedes for us with groans that words cannot express'.

6   J. Moltmann, *The Theology of Play* (New York, 1972), p. 112.

7   N. Postman, *Entertaining Ourselves To Death* (New York, 1985).

8   P. Berger, *A Rumour of Angels* (Garden City NY, 1965), esp. pp. 76–9, 118–21.

Play and laughter can be an awakening, or an epiphany, that wean us off 'The phoney ideas, cretinous people, useless products and doublespeak that increasingly dominate our lives'. I quote here from Lowe and McArthur's book *Is It Just Me or is Everything Shit?*.[9] Whilst the title of this book might cause offence, it confirms my original point regarding preoccupation with mundane creatureliness, which does not baulk at scatological matters. This 'Encyclopedia of Modern Life', as it is subtitled, reached the top ten best sellers list at WHSmith, but whilst scatology rather than eschatology – dung rather than heaven – seems to be the current preoccupation of urbanites, this juvenile whine includes the following *cri de coeur*, 'Designed for everyone who thinks they may have mislaid their soul in Coffee Republic'. Clearly, despite being seduced by consumer capitalism which melts boredom and causes hearts to leap just at the sight of shops, people still thirst for mystery and meaning – metropolitan and urban cultures are gasping for glimpses of the holy.

City dwellers – in fact all who dwell on earth – long for glimpses of the holy, because part of our human identity is to sense the holy rather than be limited to the mundane. Every one of us has a deep capacity to know and respond to a sense of the holy: this is what Thomas Aquinas refers to as *adaequatio*. We have to be confident that people, despite superficial evidence to the contrary, have an inner capacity that is adequate to perception of the presence of God, and there is mounting evidence that this is indeed the case.

Cairn Three: Risking the Possibility of Being Overwhelmed

In my first job I worked with David Hay to research the religious experience of the citizens of Nottingham. Over 250 people were interviewed and two-thirds of them were able to describe an experience where they felt they 'were aware of or influenced by a presence or power that was different from their everyday self'. As well as describing the experience, they were also invited to comment on

---

9   S. Lowe and A. McArthur, *Is It Just Me or Is Everything Shit?: The Encyclopedia of Modern Life* (London, 2005).

what they thought might have triggered that experience; the impact, both short term and long term, that it had had on them and how they made sense of the experience.[10] Interestingly, we also used the Bradburn Scale of Psychological Wellbeing to compare the levels of wellbeing of those who had had a religious experience and those who hadn't. Our work in Nottingham confirmed earlier work undertaken by Andrew Greeley in the USA. Those who reported a religious experience had a significantly higher level of psychological wellbeing than those who were unable to do so. This link with psychological wellbeing is all the more remarkable given that a quarter of those who shared their experiences in the interviews reported that they had never spoken of them prior to the interviews. Here we have the extraordinary dynamic of the persistence of religious experience alongside people's perception that in our culture there is a taboo surrounding this area of human experience.

Rather than cite statistics to justify my third cairn on the journey, I need to focus on the things that people said had triggered their religious experience. Almost without exception people reported that their religious experience had been triggered by the feeling of being powerless or at risk of being overwhelmed. However, in our risk-averse urban existence, more and more people live within their comfort zone and do their utmost to avoid such challenging and threatening circumstances. The play-pen existence of all but the poorest of city-dwellers, provides meagre support for the possibility of sensing God being alongside and accompanying and reassuring them when vulnerable and fearful. It is this inclination towards anxiety-dominated, narrow lives which has to be challenged if we are to foster openness to the holy within metropolitan men and women. So long as we operate within our capacity, we forfeit the likelihood of a transforming encounter with that which is holy.

The research I undertook with David Hay has convinced me of the significance of being brought 'face to face' with the possibility of being overwhelmed, to the occurrence of a religious experience. This

---

10   D. Hay and A. Morisy 'Secular Society? Religious Meanings: A Contemporary Paradox', *Review of Religious Research* 26 (3) 1985, pp. 213–27.

close relationship heightens the inclination of some to explain religious experience as simply a biological response to stress, but I do not think we need to be distressed by this reductive approach. To reduce religious experience to brain metabolism does not undermine the reality and impact of religious experience. The facts are that people across all cultures make sense of such experiences in terms of (their) God, or a sense of being at one with the world – an oceanic experience. Furthermore, the experience has survival value because, almost without exception, the experience brings renewed energy and heightened morale and, most significant, the experience opens the person to the needs and fragility of others. For all of us, the occurrence of a religious experience is likely to counter the inclination towards authoritarianism, foster compassion for others and reassure that 'all will be well and all manner of things will be well', to paraphrase Julian of Norwich.

It is clear that religious experience is good for people and good for society. It is a universal experience and is triggered by the feeling of being powerless or at risk of being overwhelmed, so in fostering an encounter with the sacred or holy we can harness this dynamic. That is my third cairn on the journey to constructing sacred space in the city. By creating structures or events that take people 'out of themselves' we increase the likelihood of people being without power or at risk of being overwhelmed, and in this way we can put people in the way of the holy. So a trip to Uganda to dig wells, or serving breakfast as a volunteer in a night-shelter, can play a part in communicating the holy because such participation has the capacity to denude the person of their normal coping strategies, replacing people's naive 'I'm in charge of my life' assumptions with an awareness of vulnerability and powerlessness – the effective triggers of religious experience.

Just as we can create a physical environment of peace and beauty to facilitate the perception of the holy, so too it is possible to create an emotional environment to do the same. However, the Church has traditionally been inhospitable to religious experience, preferring to limit such intimations of God's 'alongside-ness' to the occasional, usually female, saint. The Church's resistance to religious experience is understandable, because such experiences are essentially anarchic and resistant to regimentation. Religious experience is intuitive rather than formal, and most annoyingly for those who hold fast to the authority of priest and Church, religious experience is self-authenticating rather than dependent on the legitimacy granted by the formularies of the Church.

The time has come for those of us in the Church to become more accepting of religious experience, not least because one of the outcomes of an encounter with the sense of the holy or the sacred is that the person feels more 'at home' or more at ease in the world.[11] There could not be a more valuable contribution to the viability and flourishing of globalized cities than citizens who feel at home in the world and at ease with themselves and their fellows. Furthermore, the afterglow that follows the experience of the 'felt presence of God' never departs and becomes a resource to be drawn on throughout life.

Cairn Four: Engage with Tough Communal Emotions

As churches engage more and more purposefully in their communities, new opportunities emerge to encourage people to put their hopes and struggles in a wider, holier context. Opportunities for apt liturgy come about through engaging with the struggles, and on occasion the hopes, of particular communities and neighbourhoods. Encouragement to offer apt liturgy to the wider community comes from the work of Grace Davie. Her extensive research suggests that in Britain, and to a large extent in Continental Europe, we have developed 'vicarious religion', i.e. religion performed by an active minority but on behalf of a much larger number, who at some deep level are pleased that the minority are committed to maintaining a religious practice and culture.[12] This sympathy with religion is an asset in relation to creating sacred space in urban or city contexts.

Apt liturgy is different from the regular worship that takes place in

---

11   For a philosophical treatment of all these issues, see the work of H. H. Price, *Belief* (London, 1969).
12   See G. Davie, *Religion in Britain Since 1945: Believing without Belonging* (London, 1994).

church because it is designed for those who only half-believe, or have inchoate beliefs – those who are struggling with the *possibility* of God. Apt liturgy is most often designed around a distressing event, for example a fire which causes loss of life, or an outbreak of violence in the shopping precinct, or the anniversary of a war. Each community will have its own significant events, and hopefully a fair share of good events which can be celebrated. Often apt liturgy takes place outside the church building,[13] although the apt liturgy offered for the people of Soham, when faced with the murder of two young girls in their community, made good use of the church building and the symbolic resonances with eternity that the building offered.

Apt liturgy generates a feeling of solidarity between people in their struggle and it also introduces the possibility that God shares in that struggle. But more than this, apt liturgy enables some of the unequivocal aspects of the Christian faith to be shared. In helping people to embrace a sense of God being in solidarity with them, this provides an important foundation for the 'tall story' of the incarnation. Apt liturgy can often offer the balm of reassurance that all of us fall short: that to 'mess up' is the norm; that no-one is exempt because part of being human is to be vulnerable and to feel frail. By fostering this recognition, apt liturgy prepares the ground for acknowledging our need for a saviour.

Significantly, apt liturgy involves telling a story about Jesus or coming from Jesus, thus enabling the subversive perspective of Jesus to be seen, countering the popular idea that Jesus is meek and mild, appropriate for children but not for grown-ups. In a time when political ideologies are discredited, the radical way in which Jesus lived his life is both attractive and refreshing to those who find belief in a personal God difficult. Furthermore, stories about Jesus can enable a movement from struggle and dismay to that of fortitude and hope; this is an important aspect of apt liturgy. Finally, apt liturgy has the capacity to create memories of the heart that can be pondered, drawn on and built on through a lifetime. The experience of apt liturgy can

13   See A. Morisy, *Beyond the Good Samaritan.* (London, 1997), for an example of apt liturgy which takes place in a minibus.

be an epiphany – God made manifest – to those in the midst of distress and anger.

The offering of apt liturgy creates sacred space in the midst of distress, but it is an offering that calls for immense courage and emotional literacy on the part of those who design and host the liturgy or, to use more secular terminology, the event.[14] It involves identifying the situation that provokes strong emotion, acting with sensitivity, creativity and speed to offer the liturgy to those for whom religion is normally 'vicarious'. Steady commitment to community involvement is essential to achieve the alertness and prowess in responding to such opportunities; success in such initiatives will introduce people to the aptness and potency of our faith.

Cairn Five: Church Buildings Matter More and More

I have made a great deal of the holy space that can be found in church buildings. In part this is due to the growing evidence that church buildings are increasingly valued by people in general and by policy-makers at local and national level. In 2005 the Opinion Research Business Survey, sponsored by the Archbishops' Council and English Heritage, suggested that 72 per cent agreed with the statement 'a place of worship is an important part of the local community', while only 11 per cent disagreed. *Building Faith in Our Future*, a report produced by the Church Heritage Forum,[15] explored in detail how church buildings contribute positively to the life of a neighbourhood. The research commissioned by the Forum indicated that 86 per cent of the adult population had been in a church/place of worship in the previous year. This was primarily to mark social rites of passage (births, marriages and deaths) and important Christian cultural festivals (for example Christmas, Easter, Remembrance Day, Mothering Sunday) – but 19 per cent, that is one in five, were seeking a quiet space.[16]

---

14 It is worth noting that 'church' is an event before it is an organization or institution.

15 *Building Faith in Our Future* (Report of the Church Heritage Forum: London, 2004).

16 While 86 per cent had been inside a church building in the previous twelve months, only 48 per cent had been to a library, 46 per cent had been to a historic house/garden and 51 per cent had been to the cinema – Opinion Research Business (ORB) Survey, October 2003.

These data indicate that almost all adults have been in a place of worship in the last year, but what will have been communicated during that visit? We cannot be confident that we achieve a positive impact that supports an encounter with the holy. I am, at this point, reminded of a tale that the Bishop of London likes to recount. Bishop Richard, all six foot three of him, cuts a powerful image when dressed in cope and mitre and armed with a bejewelled crozier. As he is about to process into the church two youngsters shout, asking 'Who are you?' The Bishop replies 'Who do you think I am?' After a couple of seconds' delay, while the youngsters confer, the response comes: 'The Grim Reaper'. So, very much aware that there can be many a slip between intended impact and actual impact, I offer the following suggestions:

- Much of the symbolism and imagery in our churches is fine for 'adepts', who are at home in church, but less helpful for those from outside our churches who are in search of the holy. The formal symbols that we are likely to cherish often communicate the established formularies of the faith more than they purvey holiness. So beware particularly of statuary. Leave St John Vianney at home; so too St Sebastian, and Sacred Hearts are an acquired taste. City dwellers with only a meagre foundation for faith are likely to find that oddness distracts from, rather than purveys, holiness.
- Keep churches open and create a sense of the holy by appealing to the most enduring of our five senses – those of hearing and smell. These senses that remain with us even on our deathbed are the ones that entice people to venture in, to draw closer and to approach the divine.
- Keeping churches open may (not will[17]) require guardians of the holy space. Training is needed for the role of church sitting and

---

17 We assume that for a church to be open there have to be people on duty guarding the building from those with ill intent. All I can say is that I know of a number of city or urban churches that are left open without anyone on guard. This is particularly the case for churches that are run down. It is remarkable how much a state of near dereliction can pick up the mood of contemporary citizens.

welcoming. To allow the idea that the essence of the task is to protect the building and its contents is to miss the point entirely. The task is rather to hold a space where people feel safe and welcome to do business with God, and this holy hospitality is an art in which people need to be coached.

- Religious or faithful behaviour by the unlikely – the homeless person, the person with learning disabilities – can melt the hardened hearts of metropolitans. Therefore, in fostering a sense of the holy, hospitality to all comers has to be the order of the day.

- Even cool metropolitans have their hearts broken, and when a holy space is available 'per chance' then it is doubly potent; yet another reason for open churches.

- Old is cool – but complex! Historically, churches reflect the beliefs and theology of the time when they were built. Traditional, sacred architecture is often hierarchical and imposing: the traditional spire reaches upward to the heavens, carrying the message of an all powerful God located 'up in heaven'. The symbols and messages we offer need to counter this dated view, communicating both the idea of a God incarnate and that of timelessness.

- An invitation to light a candle is one way of representing the immediacy of God, but alongside the invitation it is important to give clues about the nature of prayer. The reality is that those who come to pray may be so lacking in confidence about the nature of prayer that they cannot believe it is so easy. We need to legitimize pondering and 'just sitting and thinking' as manifestations of prayerfulness. But whilst there is no need for fancy techniques in relation to prayer, the craving for 'stuff' may mean that holy objects such as rosaries, Tchotki, pearls of life and crosses all have an appeal; they give reassurance and a structure to the holy space that is offered.

- There are other ways in which old is cool. Not so long ago, I stood with a pastor from Rwanda admiring the ancient font at St Leonard's in Streatham. Together we traced the scars which showed how the font had been carefully re-assembled after a fire had destroyed the church and the font 30 years before. The

Rwandan pastor was remarkably frank. He commented that in Africa little that is old gets preserved. Few objects get venerated because of their age, and that carries an implicit message: nothing can be relied upon to last. And in turn this has a knock-on effect in relation to trust. If nothing lasts why should anyone or anything be trusted? The Rwandan Pastor's insight is relevant to the metropolitan, countering the implicit message of lives obsessed with gadgetry, in which obsolescence is routine and less and less is worth treasuring.

- Finally, old is cool because silver heads are no longer symbolic of an irrelevant past. As gridlocks and malfunctions start to dominate the horizon, silver hair signifies an admirable ability to have weathered the storms of life. Those best able to vouch for the reliability of the holy and the sacred are those who have lived a life full of ups and downs. Those in their third age, who affirm life in all its fullness, are a priceless resource in communicating the viability and sustainability of an encounter with the holy.

- Petals – mounds of them – speak of the exotic. I once found myself standing in front of the sanctuary at St Silas with an officer from the London Borough of Camden. It was during Easter week and the massive bank of lilies was before us. The local authority officer was deeply moved. He was confronted by the paltry offering that the local council made in comparison. Here was a mountain of beauty – which is how it would appear to a young child – while the offering he made to the same children was an ugly concrete structure arrayed with barbed wire and other manifestations of defensive architecture.

- Pets: I am afraid so – because to metropolitan men and women pets are on a par with people. They are preened and pampered and profitable to the ever expanding pet industry. God's grace has to extend to Tiddles and Trixie and Tyson if the holy and sacred is to be trusted. Such sentimentality is a by-product of the decadence that dominates so much of city life.

Cairn Six: The Sacred in the Hard Places in Our Cities

Not all parts of our cities can be described as metropolitan and self-indulgent. There are parts of every city where people go only reluctantly, whether as residents, or just to deliver a pizza. In every city the glamorous and pleasurable, the streets soaked with money, give way to the grey monochrome estates where the flows are those associated with drug dealing, police cars and loan sharks. What about the holy and the sacred in these contexts?

There is a church in west London that makes sure its doors are open every evening from half-past eight until ten o'clock. The doors are open for those who care about young people in that neighbourhood, particularly those youngsters who are caught up in drugs. Mums and grandparents and fathers come in and light a candle and on occasion, in that holy space, sob for the sake of their children. There is a church on the outskirts of Guildford that is open each day with the expectation that drug addicts, high on drugs, will come in. The power of the holy in that space has the potential to enable the addicted to rekindle the lost hope of being able to free themselves from their addiction; the sense of the holy in that place helps the addict to rehearse continually putting their hand in the hand of their God, as they grapple with their captivity to drugs, searching for the moment when they can say no to drugs and do say no, again and again.

In Craigmillar in Edinburgh, the church opened a café within the church building and Jessie Douglas, a local person, was employed to run the café. Jessie's son had died in a motorbike accident a year and a half before the café opened and, from its earliest days, people came in with stories from their lives – stories of children living with drug addicted parents, stories of housing difficulties and stories of loss. Stories of loss became increasingly common as the community faced a series of tragic deaths – children who had lost parents in car accidents and through suicide and murder. People began to ask if they could sit in the church for a while on their own. Eventually people asked if they could have a memorial to those who had died and a group drawn from the church and the wider community decided to make a tree out of copper piping. People learned how to weld and cut leaves out of copper sheets. The copper tree is a visual symbol of both loss and hope. Often you will find someone sitting in the church because they want to and because being there helps them. While the copper tree was being made, a boy of thirteen died in an accident at home. It was a devastating loss for his parents and five brothers and sisters. Soon afterwards, three children, Louise, Calais and Lewis, came in to the café: their parents had been killed in a road accident. From these and other experiences a second project was born, a child bereavement project called Richmond's Hope, which gives children a chance to express in therapeutic play the feelings associated with their loss.[18]

For those for whom life is unremitting in terms of grief and distress, an encounter with the holy is to gain a momentum and a motivation that can be transforming. The potency of a holy space in the midst of deeply deprived urban areas cannot be matched or replicated by other types of provision. The grace and skill to make the offering of a holy space is therefore to be harnessed especially in the raw, hardbitten and heartbroken parts of our cities.

Cairn Seven: The Power of Honest Thinking to Impart the Holy

Truth cannot be grasped by the intellect alone. There is something transcendent about truth that makes it 'totally other'. This helps explain the important relationship between the perception of the sacred and the experience and sense of truth. Truth and the process of honest thinking cannot be achieved by reason alone, because honest thinking requires more than just clarity of thought – it calls for both courage and commitment. Postmodern city dwellers are well aware that the world is too complex to fit into the neat categories of scientific formulae, analytic reports and other products of the

---

18   This story from Craigmillar is recorded in *Faithful Cities*, the Report of the Archbishops' Commission on Urban Life and Faith (London, 2006), p. 77. The account was written by the Revd Liz Henderson, Minister at Craigmillar Church.

intellect. But more than this, postmodern city dwellers have begun to detect the whiff of a pie that has gone rotten – and the even more pungent odour of denial. In such a context, the offer of honesty is a holy and sacred offering attractive to many in the city. People know in their heart of hearts that we live in the midst of tremendous dishonesty and denial, but there is an impasse, because cynicism is such that no one can be trusted to say how it is. I offer this real life story to provide some clues about who might be trusted to speak the truth.

It is a story from the churches in east Berlin, at the time when east Berlin was separated from west Berlin by the great dividing wall, fronted by furlongs of barbed wire, lit by giant arc lights and patrolled night and day. Anyone who dared to approach the wall was shot on sight. In those days the churches in east Berlin were the gathering places of tiny numbers of the lame and the halt, the very elderly, the over-emotional single women, the eccentrics. The churches were tolerated by the East German authorities, because it was clear that the churches were so weak they could be no threat to the power of the massive German Democratic Republic. Such was the feebleness of the churches the best policy was to leave them be and allow them to die of their own accord.

Except that this did not happen, because those in the churches, despite their fragility and apparent insignificance, dared to hanker after truth. They persisted in trying to read the signs of the times, and imperceptibly others began to join them. People were attracted to the honest search for truth that characterized those run-down, scorned churches, because no other agency in East Germany was prepared to acknowledge that 'the pie was rotten', that the system was not working.

What I believe happened next is not the story as you would read it in the works of the historians of modern Germany. Of course, many people and many factors did indeed play their parts in the developing drama. But, in my understanding, the prayers of those excluded people were a crucial element, all too easily neglected or denied. The broken down and often mocked churches had developed a deep prayerfulness; after all, what else could they do? Prayerfulness was the hallmark of that broken down group of people. Gradually the numbers attending the churches in east Berlin grew – and so did their prayerfulness. Prayerfulness doesn't just help us to respond humbly to the signs of the times, it also gives an extraordinary sense of timing as well. I believe that through their courageous honesty and committed prayerfulness those in the churches knew when to act; they knew when the time had come for them to begin their acts of commitment and passion, when they had to walk together, arm in arm, towards the wall, cutting back the barbed wire as they walked and wielding their sledge hammers to break down the wall.

Finding and sharing the sacred in our cities does not just mean creating a sacred garden with tumbling water cascading down rounded rocks; finding the sacred in our cities might also call for courage, for patience, for humility and for honesty, especially the honesty that dares to say 'the pie is rotten'.

A Coda for Encouragement . . .

So what good is it to create sacred space in our cities? Well, to make this offering is

- to hold out the possibility of purging us of overweening egotism . . .
- to hold out the possibility of appropriate humility . . .
- to hold out the possibility of compassion towards the stranger and to creation itself . . .
- to hold out the possibility of openness to the new and to fullness of life . . .
- to hold out the possibility of the healing of grief . . .
- to hold out the possibility of restoration of self respect and viability . . .
- to hold out the possibility of action to restore honesty to our personal and corporate actions . . .
- and to break the spell of creatureliness by restoring to us our full humanity as children of God.

For these reasons it is worth the effort to embrace the radical act of creating sacred space in our cities.

Chapter 8

Jerusalem, Dwelling of the Lord: Marian Pilgrimage and its Destination

Sarah Jane Boss

On the floor of the nave of Chartres Cathedral, there is a labyrinth. Labyrinths are not uncommon in Christian churches, and they are sometimes called 'Jerusalems', because people have supposed that the making of a devotional journey along the path of the labyrinth might have served as a substitute for the pilgrimage to Jerusalem for a would-be pilgrim who was not free to travel to the Holy Land.[1] The centre of the labyrinth, then, is a symbolic Other Jerusalem.

The journey to the Holy Land, and in particular, to Jerusalem, is indeed the prototype of Christian pilgrimage.[2] Jerusalem is the city of Mount Zion, which the Lord chose for his own dwelling; within and around its walls are the places of Our Lord's Passion, Crucifixion, Resurrection and Ascension, and the site of the descent of the Holy Spirit at Pentecost. From early centuries, Christians have visited these primordial holy places and have taken away with them relics – splinters of the true Cross, pieces of clothing worn by the Virgin Mary, or fragments of rock – so as to have something of the Holy City present in their own distant homes. All other pilgrimages should in some way approximate to this one – the journey to the principal shrine of God, which medieval cartographers placed at the centre of the world. So the pilgrimage to Jerusalem is not just the prototype, but also the archetype, of Christian pilgrimage. That is to say, it is not only the first in time and in importance, but its meaning provides the

---

1   H. Kern, *Through the Labyrinth: Designs and Meanings Over 5,000 years* (London, 2000), p. 148.

2   S. Coleman and J. Elsner, *Pilgrimage Past and Present* (London, 1995), p. 93.

structure for all other pilgrimages. And this, I suggest, is why the most popular places of pilgrimage are dedicated to the Blessed Virgin Mary. For she is the dwelling place of God incarnate – the Lord's living home, made of flesh and blood, as the Temple was his house made of stone and timber. It is said that at Chartres, the labyrinth once had at its centre a plaque bearing an image of Ariadne, the maiden whose thread was the clue that enabled Theseus to escape when he had slain the Minotaur.[3] At Chartres, the figure of Ariadne was a type of the Virgin Mary, signifying that the devotee who keeps hold of Mary during this life will reach Heaven safely. She is the guarantee of entry into the heavenly Jerusalem.

Pilgrimage and Toil

The motif of the journey is powerful in the Christian imagination. All of us are *viatores*, wayfarers on a journey whose destination we hope will be our heavenly home. And for most of human history, travel has meant hardship of one kind or another. The very word 'travel' is cognate with the word 'travail'. So the pilgrim's journey, like the Christian life, is one of hard work and endurance. Perhaps it is not surprising, then, to find that there are many places of pilgrimage which are associated with labour.

High up in the Pyrenees, in Catalonia, is the shrine of Our Lady of Núria. It is a very important pilgrimage site for Catalan people, with Núria being a popular name given to Catalan girls. Situated in a high mountain valley, the place is certainly beautiful in summer, with temperate weather, and carpeted with wild flowers. But in winter it is snowbound, and until the twentieth century was usually inaccessible for several months of the year. There is now a rack railway which connects the shrine with towns and villages lying lower in the mountains. Without the little railway, you would have to walk for a couple of hours up a very difficult track to reach the shrine from the nearest village. It

---

3   This was told to me at Chartres. Hermann Kern considers it unlikely that this labyrinth ever contained a depiction of classical figures: op. cit., p. 153.

is a spot favoured as a resting place for walkers in the summer, and it is possible to ski there in the winter. But it was only in the twentieth century that Núria took on these connotations of leisure. The origins of the shrine are pastoral. Shepherds would bring their flocks to pasture here during the months of July and August, returning to lower pasture for the winter months. According to tradition, a saint called Gil brought the Christian gospel to the valley.[4] He came and preached to the shepherds, and lived amongst them. It is said to be Gil who built the first chapel here in honour of the Mother of God. Gil tended to the shepherds' physical, as well as their spiritual, needs: he cooked food for them in a cauldron and would ring a bell to summon them from the hillsides when the food was ready for eating. The cauldron and the bell are still there, and the pilgrim is invited to put his or her head into the cauldron and to ring the bell whilst doing so – a ritual said to have the power to heal a number of infirmities and to bring other good fortune. In the chapel, there is also the wonder-working statue of Our Lady of Núria, a Romanesque Virgin in Majesty.

So the shrine of Our Lady of Núria is founded in the mundane work of shepherding flocks, and, until recently, required pilgrims to make a fairly arduous journey to reach it. A shrine with a rather similar origin is that of Our Lady of Vassivière, in the diocese of Clermont in Auvergne.[5] In winter, the statue of Our Lady lives in the church of the nearby village of Besse-en-Chandesse; but on 2 July (the old feast of the Visitation), in a procession known as *la montée*, the statue is taken up to high pastures, where the shrine of Vassivière is to be found. On 8 September, Our Lady's birthday, another procession takes the statue back down to Besse. The processional

---

4   Information about the shrine and its traditions is taken from A. H. Herce, *Vall de Núria: Libro Guía*. FGC/Vall de Núria (Barcelona, 2001); F. M. A. del Duque i Vergés, *Historia y Miracles de las Sagrad Imatge de Nostra Senyora de Nuria* [facsimile reproduction of edition of 1666] (Barcelona, 2000); *Histoire de l'Ermitage Notre-Dame de Nuria et des Principaux Miracles qui y sont opérés* [French translation of Duque i Vergés, 1867; facsimile edition]. Centre d'Estudis Comarcals del Ripollès (Ripoll, 1998).

5   An account of what can be known about this shrine from historical documents is given in C. Pourreyron, *Le Culte de Notre-Dame au Diocèse de Clermont en Auvergne* (Nancy, 1936), pp. 117–28.

calendar reflects the movement of shepherds taking flocks up to high summer pasture, and bringing them back again for the winter. Our Lady accompanied them on their journeys, and dwelt with them during their time away from home.

A Theory of 'the Sacred'

In the two examples of Núria and Vassivière, we see that sacred objects, and the journeys and rituals surrounding them, are immediately associated with daily labour and the hardship of shepherding flocks; and from a certain perspective, this might appear surprising. To consider why this is so, I turn now to the work of the great social theorist Emile Durkheim (1858–1917), one of the founding fathers of sociology and anthropology, and a major contributor to modern educational theory. Durkheim was greatly interested in religion as a social phenomenon, considering it as enormously important for social cohesion – the sharing of common values and the maintenance of a society's structure. He wrote a work entitled *The Elementary Forms of the Religious Life*, in which he tried to argue that there are certain fundamental characteristics of religious practice which can be found in all human societies. Underlying and pervading all of these is the delineation of 'the sacred' as such, in contrast to 'the mundane'. He writes that the heterogeneity between the sacred and the mundane

> is very particular: *it is absolute*. In all the history of human thought there exists no other example of things so profoundly differentiated or so radically opposed to one another. The traditional opposition of good and bad is nothing beside this; for the good and the bad are only two opposed species of the same class, namely morals, just as sickness and health are two different aspects of the same order of facts, life, while the sacred and the profane have always and everywhere been conceived by the human mind as two distinct classes, as two worlds between which there is nothing in common.[6]

---

6   E. Durkheim, *The Elementary Forms of the Religious Life* (trans. Joseph Ward Swain). (London, 1915), pp. 38–9.

Things designated as 'sacred' are distinguished and separated from common, or mundane, use. We frequently use the word 'taboo' to describe something that cannot be talked about or otherwise presented in public, and this word is borrowed from Polynesian languages, where it refers to objects withdrawn from common use and reserved for ritual use or other sacred purposes. Sacred, separated things are treated with awe, or fear, and with reverence.

Anthropologists have contested the claim that all human cultures have comparable senses of the sacred and the mundane, but Durkheim's description (although not his entire analysis) seems to fit much of the material that I examine in my own research on Christianity. For example, I have referred above to the Romanesque type of statue known as the Virgin in Majesty. This type of statue is deliberately made so that it is not true to life: the Christ-child is represented by a figure with almost adult proportions, even though he is the size of a child and seated upon his mother's lap; both mother and child are usually clothed in Roman dress, rather than the dress of the twelfth century, when most of the surviving images were carved; and the figures often have exceedingly large hands. By all these symbolic devices, the statue is marked out as 'otherworldly', as distinct from the everyday world.[7] Likewise, church architecture has often been quite different in form and decoration from domestic architecture; and this is not only for functional reasons (e.g., the need to accommodate a large congregation and perform certain ritual actions), but in order to create something that will inspire awe and devotion in the worshipper, or to incorporate sacred symbols into a building that is for sacred use. Again, by blessing themselves with holy water on entering and leaving a church, worshippers signal that they are crossing the threshold between the sacred and the mundane.

Durkheim himself was a Frenchman from a devout Jewish family.[8] His father was a rabbi, and I suspect that much of Durkheim's think-

---

7 A brief account of this type of statue can be found in S. J. Boss, *Mary* (London, 2004), pp. 105–18.
8 S. Lukes, *Emile Durkheim: His Life and Work: A Historical and Critical Study* (Harmondsworth, 1973), p. 39.

ing about human society, and religion in particular, was greatly influenced by that upbringing. Perhaps it is not surprising to find that in Jewish Sabbath prayers, there is a prayer which addresses God as the one who 'distinguishes between the holy and the mundane, between light and darkness, between Israel and the nations, between the seventh day and the six days of creation'. It finishes: 'Blessed are you, O God, who distinguish between the holy and the mundane'. So we can see that whilst Durkheim, the secular sociologist, taught that the separation of the sacred from the mundane was something done by human beings for reasons of social cohesion, the religious background from which he came had tried to teach him that this distinction was decreed by God as part of the order of creation.

At the beginning of the book of Genesis, we read that, when God first created the heavens and the earth, 'the earth was without form and void'. Jewish and Christian thinkers through the ages have asked what this phrase really means. There have been many different interpretations of the expression 'formless and void', and I want to point out just one of them. The Hebrew phrase which is translated as 'formless and void' is *tohu vavohu*. In English, there used to be a word derived from the Hebrew, and the English was 'tohu-bohu', meaning 'muddled, confused, higgledy piggledy, chaotic'. Now some philosophers have argued that in the beginning what God made was chaos, and that the work of creation was then a work of separating things out from the chaos, of differentiating things, so that each thing could have its own identity – so that each thing could have its proper relationships to other things. God's continuing work of creation is thus one of ensuring that things are not confused. William James, author of the seminal work *The Varieties of Religious Experience*, says that a new-born baby experiences the world as a 'buzzing, blooming mass', and that through its progressive interactions with the world around it, the baby gradually learns to sort things out. The infant learns that things have their own identities, and it is language which is the principal medium for this establishing of identities. Words not only designate, but, in the human mind, help to create, discrete objects and relationships. And perhaps James's idea is a very ancient one, for in Genesis 1 we read that it is through *words* – through *speech*

– that God causes order to emerge out of chaos. 'God said, "Let there be light", and there was light', and the light was separated from darkness; and so on for the six days of creation.

It follows that part of what it is to live a good life is to show respect for God's ordering of creation. Thus, Catholics have a strong tradition of natural law, according to which God has ordered the world in a particular way such that human moral law can and should be in accordance with the order of creation. Jewish rules about not mixing certain foodstuffs, and not making fabrics from mixed fibres, may be seen as a more refined interpretation of the same basic principle. Now, one aspect of the divine ordering of things is the separation of the sacred from the mundane. In the Genesis narrative, this is seen in the creation of the Sabbath day, which is quite distinct from the six days that have preceded it, although the creation of the mundane world is itself a part of the sacred order of things. So for both Jews and most Christians, it is important to show proper reverence for that which is set aside as sacred. We mark out times of fasting and penitence, such as Lent and Advent; we have times for feasting, with the giving of gifts and abstaining from work, as at Easter and Christmas; we honour sacred places, such as churches and pilgrimage sites, by adopting distinct codes of behaviour in our speech, our dress and our mannerisms; and we have sacred objects, such as the communion host, which is handled differently from other food – it is not put in the larder or the pocket, for example – and is consumed as part of a different ritual from that of other meals.

Let us return, then, to the shrines of Núria and Vassivière. In these two examples, we find that things that are sacred – the holy image and the rituals surrounding it – are immediately associated with mundane work, that of shepherding flocks. Sacred actions, far from being separated from the mundane, were once completely tied in to the working lives of shepherds. And we can think of more examples of this bonding of the sacred to the workaday. The Church calendar follows the movement of the sun through the heavens, which is to say that it also follows the agricultural and pastoral year. Thus, Candlemas, on 2 February, was once the time for the blessing of the fields and the start of ploughing. Lammas, the first Sunday of August, was once the time for the blessing of the first loaves, and was followed by a fortnight of harvest celebration, culminating in the feast of the Assumption on 15 August. In some parts of England, the traditional wakes weeks still fall within this period. Here again, the time designated as sacred is linked to time that is defined by labouring. This raises the question as to whether the whole idea that the sacred is necessarily distinguished from the mundane might not be mistaken.

The Exception which Proves the Rule

Let us approach the subject, then, from a different angle. So far, I have spoken mainly of a particular sociological account of the sacred. I have referred to human practices of separating particular times, places and objects, and to treating them with fear and reverence. However, I have also observed that a particular religious account of this separation views it primarily not as something done by humans, but as something ordained by God. Yet what would be God's purpose in distinguishing within the creation between that which is sacred and that which is mundane? Well, from a theological point of view, I suggest that something is properly called 'sacred' either when God is present in it, or else when God reveals 'Godself' in it in some distinctive manner. For example, the liturgical celebration of Easter is sacred because it is the occasion when the Lord's Resurrection is revealed to us with a special vividness. A stronger instance of the sacred would be the eucharist: God is present in the eucharistic host in a special way because of a particular dispensation going back to Christ during his ministry on earth. The anthropologists Victor Turner and Edith Turner argue, in a well known study of Christian pilgrimage, *Image and Pilgrimage in Christian Culture*, that a principal characteristic of a pilgrim shrine – such as Jerusalem, Lourdes or Walsingham – is that the veil between heaven and earth is slightly pulled aside, so that the pilgrim gains a little glimpse of the Other World, the Heavenly Realm.[9] We could see pilgrim shrines as an example of what neo-pagans

9   This notion is expanded in V. Turner and E. Turner, *Image and Pilgrimage in Christian Culture* (Oxford, 1978), pp. 1–39.

sometimes designate as 'thin places'. At a holy place, God is revealed in some exceptional way, with healings or other miracles being the plainest revelations of this kind.

I was brought up as a Quaker, a member of the Religious Society of Friends, and a distinctive feature of Friends' practice is that no times, no places and no objects are set aside as holy, because all things are deemed to be equally sacred. The reasoning here is that if certain days are set aside as holy days, if churches are set aside as holy places, liturgical communion as a holy meal, and monks, nuns and priests as holy people, then all other times, places, meals and people are implicitly judged to be profane. Friends, however, believe in the holiness of all things. They say, 'Every day is Easter day; every meal is a communion', and for that reason they do not have a liturgical calendar, or priests, or consecrated buildings. Now, like the members of the Society of Friends, I believe that God is indeed present in all times, places and people, and that we ought to treat all with reverence. But one reason why I left the Society of Friends was that it became clear to me that in order to know what it is for something to be holy, we have to have exemplars of holiness. If you have never been to a church celebration of Easter, how do you know what it means to say, 'Every day is Easter day'? If you have never been to a liturgical communion, how do you know what it means to say, 'Every meal is a communion'? It is by going to holy places (I think here particularly of Wells Cathedral, Stonehenge, Tewkesbury Abbey, or the Malvern Hills) that I learn what it means for a place to be holy. I can then return to my own home and try to find or create that holiness there as well. It was partly considerations of this kind that led to my becoming a Catholic.

My own attitude, I discovered, has a long pedigree in the Christian tradition. The Rule of St Benedict enjoins its followers to treat the objects that they use for work – pots and pans, knives and spades – as if they were the sacred vessels on the altar. Even the humblest of things should be treated with reverence. But we need to have the example of sacred vessels to know what is being asked of us in relation to pots and pans.

God's separation of the sacred from the mundane, then, is not a

designation of the latter as worthless. Quite the contrary: it is a separation which enables us to see the true holiness of the whole created
order. The shepherds who took their flocks on the long trek up to
Núria every summer lived cheek by jowl with a holy shrine and its
legends, and with the sacred statue of the mother of God. And I have
no doubt that the code of conduct which governed their behaviour
in the church and the shrine was rather different from that which
governed their conduct towards one another, especially during their
leisure time. It seems unlikely that they were ever the romantic
figures of an eighteenth-century pastoral idyll, and they probably
reserved their best behaviour for going to church and saying their
prayers. Yet perhaps the fact that they had that frequent experience of
venerating the mother of God – the one who bore God in her own
body – meant that when they turned to one another, they could
sometimes see the presence of God in a fellow shepherd and in the
earth which gave them their livelihood, and could know the strength
and tenderness of God in their daily hardships.

The mysterious contrast and connection between the sacred and
the mundane runs more deeply than the level of human psychology.
The distinction between the sacred and the mundane is not just a
device by which God reminds us of the holiness of all creation;
rather, the hardships by which we know the extent of our exclusion
from paradise are the very means by which we long for, and eventually attain, our heavenly goal. When Adam and Eve were expelled
from the Garden of Eden, Adam was burdened with having to toil
with the sweat of his brow in order to gain a living, as did the shepherds of the Núria valley; and so was Eve with enduring the pains of
childbirth, as undoubtedly did the shepherds' wives and mothers.
The expulsion from Eden was the beginning of humanity's trials and
tribulations and, according to the most commonly narrated form of
the story, from here began the journey of all creation towards salvation – that is, the restoration of paradise, or the attainment of the
heavenly Jerusalem, the Kingdom of God. Men and women have
always sought out holy things: holy places, holy times, holy objects.
These offer that foretaste of the final heavenly state that is our proper
home. Yet perhaps Adam and Eve knew what is sacred only by

contrast with what is mundane, and their hardships are both the setting and the means of their sanctification – of their preparation for Heaven. A pilgrimage can be seen as the whole human story in microcosm, and that is part of the meaning of the sufferings which the pilgrim traditionally endures on the way.

So let us consider the fact that the single largest group of pilgrimages in the world are to sites dedicated to the Blessed Virgin Mary. The shrine of Our Lady of Guadalupe in Mexico City receives up to fifteen million visitors each year, and Lourdes receives five million. This is partly for economic reasons. Europeans and North Americans are richer than people in other parts of the world and can afford to travel long distances. Also, these are shrines traditionally visited all year round rather than only on particular feasts – another factor which tends to increase the total number of visitors. However, the number of local pilgrimage sites dedicated to Mary is also phenomenally large throughout Europe, and many countries' national and regional shrines are Marian: Einsiedeln in Switzerland; Czestochowa in Poland; Saragossa, together with Compostela, in Spain; Altötting in Bavaria; Montserrat in Catalonia; and so on. All these are pilgrimage destinations. So why is Marian pilgrimage the most popular form of pilgrimage? Why are the journeys of Christian pilgrims so commonly directed to places consecrated to the Mother of God? Well, in the light of the observation that I have already made to the effect that pilgrimage is a microscosm of the soul's journey towards Heaven, we can note that, in Mary, the holiness which fits us for Heaven is fully accomplished. She is the emblem of that which we are striving to become, and the guarantee that such holiness is possible in a human person. But more than this, I suggest, Mary embodies the state of paradise, because she has been the living shrine of God incarnate. As Robert Southwell writes in his poem, 'The Virgine Maries conception', 'Earth breeds heaven/for God's new dwelling place'.[10] As the Mother of God, Mary is the Temple who houses the Lord: she has

---

10   R. Southwell, 'The Virgine Maries conception', *Poems of Robert Southwell SJ*, eds J. H. McDonald and N. P. Brown (Oxford, 1967), p. 3. The poem is also known as 'The Conception of Our Lady'.

been Heaven on earth, and in the places that are sacred to her, she again guarantees lodging to her divine Son. When we travel to Mary, we find the presence of God. Indeed, the converse is also true: whenever we meet Christ, we meet him in Mary, because she is the heavenly state whom God created to be his own dwelling.

In the light of the connection between the sacred and the mundane which I have described above, it is only to be expected that the woman whom millions of people travel and struggle to find in her remote shrines is also honoured in the mass-produced rosaries which they carry every day in their pockets, or the Miraculous Medals which they tie to a baby's cot, or the routine Hail Marys which are said over and over again with little thought. I once fell into conversation with a working-class woman from Liverpool who was a very devout Catholic. When I told her that my work focused on Marian theology and devotion, she immediately exclaimed, 'Oh, I love Our Lady!' She then said, 'I talk to Our Lady all the time. When I go shopping, I say, "Come on, Our Lady, let's go shopping!"' And she laughed, as though recognizing that I might think there was something quirky about this kind of chit-chat with the Blessed Virgin Mary. Then suddenly, the woman's face changed. She looked very serious and said, 'And you know, she's up there with the Blessed Trinity. She's really powerful!' This woman's sense of the Virgin Mary as someone who is both so ordinary that you can ask her to go shopping with you and at the same time so highly honoured that she is closest to God and the possessor of extraordinary supernatural power, articulates perfectly the position of Mary in the scheme of salvation. As the Word of God, through whom the universe was created, chose to take the human condition upon himself, so the woman who gave him his humanity has been raised up to the loftiest place in the company of Heaven, at the side of her eternal Son. The connection between the heavenly and the workaday is concretely established in the Incarnation.

Knowing Sanctity through Hardship

It is clear, then, that there is a contrast and a bond between daily toil and the sacred goal of human life, and that the office of Mother of God pervades that relationship. Let us look more closely, then, at the significance of this 'daily toil'.

The shepherds and shepherdesses who took their flocks to graze in Núria and Vassivière were not just 'doing their job': their work was not merely mundane, as is a job in, say, an insurance company. They were engaged in activities necessary for basic human survival. Their sheep provided meat for food, wool for clothing and hides for leather. Furthermore, the conditions in which the shepherds laboured were sufficiently harsh for them to have been frequently reminded of their own bare physical needs. And perhaps it is for this reason that the places of high summer pasture became known as sacred. For knowledge of the sacred, of the spiritual, and of heavenly things is given to us precisely in states of physical necessity. Indeed, is this not the very reason for the traditional hardships of pilgrimage?

A pilgrim route that is famous for making tough demands on its travellers is that of Santiago de Compostela, in north-western Spain. It is associated especially with St James, who is the Apostle to Spain, but for hundreds of years was popular with pilgrims from all over Europe. There was no route to Santiago that did not entail a long and dangerous journey and, as with most pilgrimages, the journey was undertaken in order to acquire spiritual merit, such as atonement for sin, either for oneself or on behalf of someone else. In recent years, there has been a great revival of this pilgrimage, with thousands of people from Europe and North America – some of them Christians, some of them just seekers after spiritual truth – walking or cycling across the whole of northern Spain. The pilgrimage is deemed not to count as such if it is undertaken by car or by train, so the element of hardship is integral to the undertaking.

A woman from west Wales, whom I shall refer to as 'Clare', has spoken of her own experience of this pilgrimage. She had a son who died unexpectedly in his teens, and Clare got together with other bereaved mothers to form a group who made the pilgrimage together to Santiago. So these women started out as a group who were emotionally wounded and exposed, and they undertook a journey that was physically tough and exhausting. Clare described the austerity of many of the lodging houses along the way: a room with twenty bunk beds in it, one toilet, and only cold water to wash in. Local volunteers would come to provide hot food from a big pot for the weary travellers. But to the exhausted pilgrims, the delight of finding a bed to lie in, water with which to wash, and a meal to eat made this basic accommodation a joy to arrive at. Clare described how a sense of the holiness of things was greatly intensified by the state of necessity – by the awareness of one's need for food, water, sleep and the companionship of one's fellow pilgrims. It was in this state of neediness that the pilgrim could discern most clearly the presence of God along her route.

Most people finish the pilgrimage to Santiago at the cathedral of Santiago de Compostela. However, the traditional pilgrim route led beyond this point, to Finisterra on the Atlantic coast, where there is a shrine dedicated to the Blessed Virgin Mary. Clare and one of her companions made this last part of the pilgrimage and it was by far the most difficult. Yet Clare said that reaching Finisterra was by far the most important part of her journey, both spiritually and for the emotional healing that had been an essential part of the women's journey from the outset.

Throughout the world, holy men and women – such a St Gil of Núria – have chosen to live lives of poverty in remote places, because it is when we are aware of our most basic necessities that we are most open to the presence of God. Perhaps this is one reason why Christ says that the poor are blessed: they do not have material possessions, but they are able to acquire spiritual treasures, whilst we who are rich have already received our transient reward.

Very unlike the pilgrimage to Santiago, however, are most pilgrimages to Lourdes. This was once a relatively remote town in the French Pyrenees, but modern communications ensure that it is now quite easily accessible. In 1858, a poor girl names Bernadette Soubirous had a series of visions in the grotto of Massabielle, just outside the town of Lourdes. In the visions, she saw and heard a white figure who eventually identified herself as 'the Immaculate Conception', and thus as the Virgin Mary. The lady of the vision directed Bernadette to dig in the mud with her hands, as a result of which she uncovered a spring which turned out to have healing properties.[11] Lourdes was rapidly promoted as a pilgrim shrine,[12] and today receives tens of thousands of visitors every week during the summer, and smaller numbers the whole year round. The modern journey to Lourdes could not be more different from that to Santiago. Trains, coaches and planes transport people rapidly to hotels of every standard, according to the pilgrims' ability and willingness to pay. Yet if we ask who are the people who travel to Lourdes, the question of speed and comfort takes on a somewhat different aspect. For many of the pilgrims are very ill or handicapped and may have been advised by doctors not to travel at all. For them, the journey to Lourdes is physically as tough as that of the healthy pilgrim walking the road to Compostela. Moreover, many of the pilgrims are people whose lives are already dominated by physical necessity: they need help with the most basic tasks, such as getting dressed or going to the toilet, whilst others have life-threatening illnesses. The able-bodied people who go to Lourdes to help those who are sick and handicapped often describe their own experience of the pilgrimage as one of totally exhausting hard work but, at the same time, as an occasion of enormous grace and joy. Pilgrims of all kinds typically say that Lourdes is an exceptionally holy place where they feel at peace and know the presence of God.[13]

---

11   The best biography of Bernadette Soubirous, which recounts the apparitions and the discovery of the shrine in detail, is: T. Taylor, *Bernadette of Lourdes: Her Life, Death and Visions* (London, 2003). For a shorter account of Bernadette's visions and other Marian apparitions, see S. Zimdars-Swartz, *Encountering Mary: Visions of Mary from La Salette to Medjugorje* (Princeton, NJ, 1991).

12   The history of the origins and development of the shrine at Lourdes is given in R. Harris, *Lourdes: Body and Spirit in the Secular Age* (London, 1991).

13   A. Dahlberg, *Transcendence of Bodily Suffering: An Anthropological Study of English Catholics at Lourdes*, PhD Thesis, London School of Economic and Political Science, 1987. A summary of a section of this thesis is published as 'The Body as a Principle of Holism: Three pilgrimages to Lourdes', in J. Eade and M. J. Sallnow, *Contesting the Sacred: The Anthropology of Christian Pilgrimage* (London, 1991), pp. 30–50.

In conditions in which we are aware of physical necessity, God gives us a sense of the sacred and so increases our desire for him; and in desiring God, we transcend the very conditions of hardship in which we were first led into that desire. An awareness of the sacred is a sense of the closeness of God, and Mary is the archetype of all places where the sacred can be known because Christ dwells within her. At a holy place, we enter a Marian space and in our intimacy with Christ, his divinity transforms our humanity beyond the weakness which made us know our need of him.

It should be a cause of great concern to Christians that we live in a society in which many people are cut off from the experience of basic physical necessity. We buy goods that are processed, packaged and delivered over long distances, so that we do not know what they are made of or how they are made. People are born in hospitals and die in hospitals, away from everyday life. The basic stuff of our lives is hidden from us. And it is not only the material, but also the spiritual, foundation that is hidden from us. In a world in which people can forget that food is grown in soil, and that it depends upon rain and sun, it is no accident that they have also forgotten that our lives come from God, that they depend upon God, and that they are returning to God. A sense of God is natural to human beings; and just as we have forgotten that our nature is physical, so we have also forgotten that our nature is spiritual. Yet this detachment from physical necessity is, in the end, an illusion. We are all vulnerable to illness, injury and death. And the Christian gospel of hope tells us that it is in that most dire necessity, death, that God will be most fully present to us. St Cyril of Alexandria (d. 444), one of the greatest theologians of the Incarnation, teaches that because the immortal Word of God united him to human flesh even in death, he accomplished 'the incorruptibility and imperishability of the flesh . . . , first of all in his own body', as is seen in his own Resurrection, but also for the whole human race. For by uniting himself to human death in Christ, God who is immortal overcame death itself and thus enabled all flesh to be 'set . . . beyond death and corruption'.[14] 'In short, he

---

14   St Cyril of Alexandria, *On the Unity of Christ*, trans. A. J. McGuckin (New York, 1995), p. 57.

took what was ours to be his very own so that we might have all that was his'.[15]

In many of the world's cultures, death is the most unholy, the most impure state of all. Yet in Christianity, the all-holy God took this very state upon himself and in so doing, overcame profane death with sacred immortality. If we do not allow ourselves to know our own weakness, vulnerability and mortality, how are we to become aware of the God who redeems and transforms that same weakness and mortality? The pilgrim to Jerusalem goes to the place which God had chosen to be his special dwelling from ancient times; to the places where the union of God and humanity occurred in Jesus Christ – where deity was bound to a human infant in its birth and to a human man in his death and resurrection. Like the Temple of Solomon, Mary is the Lord's earthly seat and all those who make pilgrimages to 'other Jerusalems' enter a Marian space in which, if we know our human frailty, we will also know the gift of Christ breathing into us the Spirit of eternal life.

---

15   Ibid., p. 59.

Bibliography

Alberti, L. B., *Ten Books on Architecture*, ed. and trans. J. Leoni (London, 1955).

Alves, Rubem M., *A Theology of Human Hope* (Washington, 1969).

Barker, M., *The Great Angel: A Study of Israel's Second God* (London, 1992).

Barker, M., *The Great High Priest* (London and New York, 2003).

Barker, M., 'Justinian's New Church and the Entry of the Mother of God into the Temple', in *Sourozh. A Journal of Orthodox Life and Thought*, 103 (2006), pp. 15–33.

Barth, Karl, *Church Dogmatics*, 1.2 (Edinburgh, 1956).

Beard, M., North, J. and Price, S., *Religions of Rome* (2 vols, Cambridge, 1998).

Berger, Peter L., *A Rumour of Angels: Modern Society and the Rediscovery of the Supernatural* (Garden City NY, 1969).

Boss, Sarah Jane, *Mary* (London, 2004).

Bouyer, Louis, *Life and Liturgy* (London, 1956).

Boyle, Nicholas, *Sacred and Secular Scriptures: A Catholic Approach to Literature* (London, 2004).

Brown, M. P., '"In the Beginning was the Word": Books and Faith in the Age of Bede', *Jarrow Lecture* (2000).

Brown, M. P., *The Lindisfarne Gospels: Society, Spirituality and the Scribe* (Luzern, London and Toronto, 2003).

Brown, M. P., 'An Early Outbreak of "Influenza"? Aspects of Influence, Medieval and Modern', in A. Bovey, ed., *Under the Influence: the concept of influence and the study of illuminated manuscripts* (Turnhout, 2005).

Brown, M. P., *How Christianity Came to Britain and Ireland* (Oxford, 2006).

Brown, M. P., *Manuscripts from the Anglo-Saxon Age* (London and Toronto, 2006).

Brown, M. P., *The Luttrell Psalter* (London, 2006).

Building Faith in Our Future, (Report of the Church Heritage Forum, London, 2004).

Coleman, Simon and Elsner, John, *Pilgrimage Past and Present* (London, 1995).

Dahlberg, Andrea, 'The Body as a Principle of Holism: Three Pilgrimages to Lourdes', in Eade, John and Sallnow, Michael J., *Contesting the Sacred: The Anthropology of Christian Pilgrimage* (London, 1991).

Davie, Grace, *Religion in Britain Since 1945: Believing without Belonging* (London, 1994).

Duby, Georges, *The Age of the Cathedrals*, English translation of *Le temps des cathédrals* (London, 1981).

Duffy, Eamon, *The Stripping of the Altars* (New Haven, 1992).

Durkheim, Emile, *The Elementary Forms of the Religious Life*, trans. Joseph Ward Swain (London, 1915).

Elie, P., *The Life You Have May Be Your Own: An American Pilgrimage* (New York, 2003).

Faithful Cities, The Report of the Archbishops' Commission on Urban Life and Faith (London, 2006).

Harris, Ruth, *Lourdes: Body and Spirit in the Secular Age* (London, 1991).

Hay, David and Morisy, Ann, 'Secular Society? Religious Meanings: A Contemporary Paradox', *Review of Religious Research* 26 (3), pp. 213–27.

Inge, John, *A Christian Theology of Place* (London, 2003).

Jennings, E. (ed.), *In Praise of Our Lady* (London, 1982).

Josipovici, Gabriel, *The Book of God: A Response to the Bible* (New Haven, 1988).

Kern, Hermann, *Through the Labyrinth: Designs and Meanings over 5,000 years* (London, 2000).

Kletter, R., 'Between Archaeology and Theology. The Pillar Figurines from Judah and the Asherah', in A. Mazar (ed.), *Studies in the*

Archaeology of the Iron Age in Israel and Jordan (Sheffield, 2001), pp. 179–216.

Lukes, Steven, *Emile Durkheim: His Life and Work: A Historical and Critical Study* (Harmondsworth, 1973).

Marcuse, Herbert, *One Dimensional Man: Studies in the Ideology of Advanced Industrial Society* (Boston, 1964).

Mission-Shaped Church: Church Planting and Fresh Expressions of Church in a Changing Context (Church of England Mission and Public Affairs Council (London, 2004).

Moltmann, Jürgen, *The Theology of Play* (New York, 1972).

Morisy, Ann, *Beyond the Good Samaritan* (London, 1997).

Nordenfalk, C., *Studies in the History of Book Illumination* (London, 1992).

O'Reilly, J., 'The Library of Scripture: Views from the Vivarium and Wearmouth-Jarrow', in P. Binski and W. G. Noel (eds), *New Offerings, Ancient Treasures: Essays in Medieval Art for George Henderson* (Stroud, 2001).

Postman, Neil, *Entertaining Ourselves To Death* (New York, 1985).

Powys, A. R., *The English Parish Church* (London, 1930).

Price, H. H., *Belief* (London, 1969).

Pritchard, Stephen, *Words and The Word* (Cambridge, 1986).

Ramsey, A. M., *From Gore to Temple* (London, 1960).

Rolheiser, Ronald, *The Shattered Lantern* (New York, 1997).

Rowland, Christopher, 'Friends of Albion', in S. Platten and C. Lewis (eds), *Flagships of the Spirit: Cathedrals in Society* (London, 1998).

Sayers, Dorothy L., *The Man Born to be King* (London, 1943).

Schönborn, C., *God's Human Face* (San Francisco, 1994).

Skehan, P. S., 'A Fragment of the Song of Moses (Deut 32) from Qumran', *Bulletin of the American Schools of Oriental Research* 136 (1954), pp. 12–14.

Stephenson, Colin, *Walsingham Way* (London, 1970).

Taylor, J., *Christians and the Holy Places* (Oxford, 1993).

Taylor, Thérèse, *Bernadette of Lourdes: Her Life, Death and Visions* (London, 2003).

Temple, William, *Nature, Man, and God* (London, 1935).

Torrance, T. F., *Space, Time and Incarnation* (London, New York, Toronto, 1969).

Turner, Victor and Turner, Edith, *Image and Pilgrimage in Christian Culture* (Oxford, 1978).

van Seters, J., 'The Religion of the Patriarchs in Genesis', *Biblica* 6 (1) (1980), pp. 220–33.

Walker, Peter, *Holy City, Holy Places* (Oxford, 1990).

Walker, Peter (ed.), *Jerusalem Past and Present in the Purposes of God* (Carlisle, 1992).

White, Susan, 'The Theology of Sacred Space', in A. Loades and D. Brown (eds), *The Sense of the Sacramental* (London, 1995), pp. 31–43.